Developing
Your Child's Potential

By the Editors of Time-Life Books

Alexandria, Virginia

TIME ®
LIFE
BOOKS

Time-Life Books Inc.
is a wholly owned subsidiary of

Time Incorporated

FOUNDER: Henry R. Luce 1898-1967

Editor-in-Chief: Henry Anatole Grunwald
Chairman and Chief Executive Officer:
J. Richard Munro
President and Chief Operating Officer:
N. J. Nicholas Jr.
Chairman of the Executive Committee:
Ralph P. Davidson
Corporate Editor: Ray Cave
Executive Vice President, Books: Kelso F. Sutton
Vice President, Books: George Artandi

Time-Life Books Inc.

EDITOR: George Constable
Director of Design: Louis Klein
Director of Editorial Resources: Phyllis K. Wise
Acting Text Director: Ellen Phillips
Editorial Board: Russell B. Adams Jr., Dale M.
Brown, Roberta Conlan, Thomas H. Flaherty, Donia
Ann Steele, Rosalind Stubenberg, Kit van Tulleken,
Henry Woodhead
Director of Photography and Research:
John Conrad Weiser

PRESIDENT: Christopher T. Linen
Executive Vice President: John M. Fahey Jr.
Senior Vice Presidents: James L. Mercer,
Leopoldo Toralballa
Vice Presidents: Stephen L. Bair, Ralph J. Cuomo,
Terence J. Furlong, Neal Goff, Stephen L. Goldstein,
Juanita T. James, Hallett Johnson III, Robert H.
Smith, Paul R. Stewart
Director of Production Services:
Robert J. Passantino

Library of Congress Cataloguing in
Publication Data
Developing your child's potential.
  (Successful parenting)
  Bibliography: p.
  Includes index.
  1. Education, Preschool — Parent participation. 2.
Child development. I. Time-Life Books. II. Series.
LB1140.35.P37D48 1987   649'.68   86-23130
ISBN 0-8094-5929-9
ISBN 0-8094-5930-2 (lib. bdg.)

Successful Parenting

SERIES DIRECTOR: Donia Ann Steele
Deputy Editor: Jim Hicks
Series Administrator: Norma E. Shaw
Editorial Staff for *Developing Your Child's Potential:*
Designer: Cynthia Richardson
Picture Editor: Jane Jordan
Text Editor: Robert A. Doyle
Staff Writer: Janet Cave
Researchers: Charlotte Fullerton, Karen Monks,
Mark Moss (principals), Fran Moshos,
Nancy C. Scott
Copy Coordinators: Marfé Ferguson,
Carolee Belkin Walker
Picture Coordinator: Bradley Hower
Editorial Assistant: Jenester C. Lewis

Special Contributors: Amy Goodwin Aldrich,
Charlotte Anker, Lynn Crawford, George Daniels,
Pat Daniels, Michael Durham, Clare Grosegebauer,
Marilyn Humm, Ray Jones, Phyllis Lehmann-
McIntosh, Brian McGinn, Martin Mann, John
Manners, Brian Miller, Carolyn Mooney, James G.
Moore, Wendy Murphy, Barbara Palmer, Susan
Perry, Gerry Schremp, William Worsley, Enid
Yurman (text); Laura Boudreaux, Julia Brent,
Patricia Cassidy-Lewis, Jill Denny, Anne Munoz
Furlong, Melva Holloman, Brandi McDougall, Gail
Prensky, Beth Py (research); Jennifer Gilman
(design).

Editorial Operations
Copy Chief: Diane Ullius
Editorial Operations: Caroline A. Boubin
(manager)
Production: Celia Beattie
Library: Louise D. Forstall

Correspondents: Elisabeth Kraemer-Singh (Bonn);
Maria Vincenza Aloisi (Paris); Ann Natanson
(Rome).

First printing. Printed in U.S.A.

Published simultaneously in Canada.
School and library distribution by
Silver Burdett Company, Morristown,
New Jersey 07960.

TIME-LIFE is a trademark of Time
Incorporated U.S.A.

Other Publications

FIX IT YOURSELF
FITNESS, HEALTH & NUTRITION
HEALTHY HOME COOKING
UNDERSTANDING COMPUTERS
LIBRARY OF NATIONS
THE ENCHANTED WORLD
THE KODAK LIBRARY OF CREATIVE PHOTOGRAPHY
GREAT MEALS IN MINUTES
THE CIVIL WAR
PLANET EARTH
COLLECTOR'S LIBRARY OF THE CIVIL WAR
THE EPIC OF FLIGHT
THE GOOD COOK
WORLD WAR II
HOME REPAIR AND IMPROVEMENT
THE OLD WEST

*For information on and a full description of any
of the Time-Life Books series listed above, please
write:*
Reader Information
Time-Life Books
541 North Fairbanks Court
Chicago, Illinois 60611

This volume is one of a series about raising children.

The Consultants

General Consultants

Dr. Dorothy G. Singer, an authority on mental development in young children, is Professor of Psychology at the University of Bridgeport in Connecticut and former director of the university's School Psychology Program. Dr. Singer is also a research affiliate at the Yale University Child Study Center and serves as codirector of Yale's Family Television Research and Consultation Center, where she has supervised projects aimed at stimulating imaginative development in preschool children. She is co-author of *A Piaget Primer: How a Child Thinks; Teaching Television: How to Use Television to Your Child's Advantage;* and *Make Believe: Games and Activities to Foster Imaginative Play in Young Children.*

Dr. Joseph Sparling is an expert on early childhood education and on the role of play in young children's learning. As a senior research investigator at the Frank Porter Graham Child Development Center of the University of North Carolina at Chapel Hill, he has done considerable work in preschool curriculum development and is currently evaluating the effectiveness of preschool programs in enhancing intellectual growth. Dr. Sparling has developed educational toys for young children, and he has written articles for *Parents* and *Redbook* magazines. His published work includes *Learningames for the First Three Years, Learningames for Threes and Fours* and *Partners for Learning.*

Special Consultants

Dr. Walter C. Allan, a pediatric neurologist, advised on the section concerning the child's brain and how its development affects learning abilities. Dr. Allan has researched and published numerous articles on the nervous sytem of infants, and he has a special interest in how the brain matures. He is in private practice, associated with the Maine Medical Center in Portland.

Dr. Sylvia Feinburg, an associate professor at the Eliot-Pearson Department of Child Study at Tufts University, contributed to the essay on the developmental stages of children's art, providing the original drawings from her extensive personal collection spanning 35 years. Dr. Feinburg has written and lectured widely on the subject of how a child's art parallels his cognitive and emotional development. She has trained art educators and child development specialists, and she has planned art education curricula for schools and day-care centers.

Dr. James J. Gallagher, who assisted with the essay on gifted children, is Director of the Frank Porter Graham Child Development Center and a professor of education at the University of North Carolina at Chapel Hill. A former president of the World Council for Gifted and Talented Children, Dr. Gallagher is the editor of the *Journal for the Education of the Gifted* and the author of *Teaching the Gifted Child.*

Dr. David L. Gallahue, a specialist on childhood motor development, contributed to the section on suggested activities for strengthening physical skills. He is a professor of physical education and Dean of Research and Development in the School of Health, Physical Education and Recreation at Indiana University at Bloomington, and he is the author of *Developmental Physical Education of Today's Children* and *Understanding Motor Development in Children.*

Dr. Doris J. Johnson, who helped develop the section on conditions that hinder learning, heads the Program in Learning Disabilities at Northwestern University. She is the chairman of the Professional Advisory Board of the Association for Children with Learning Disabilities and is affiliated with the International Academy for Research in Learning Disabilities. She has lectured in this country and abroad, and she has published numerous articles on the subject of educating children who have learning disorders.

Dr. Jerome Kagan, who gave his expert view on the resilient nature of children, is a psychologist recognized worldwide for his contributions to the understanding of intellectual and emotional growth. A professor of human development at Harvard University, Dr. Kagan is the recipient of two prestigious honors in his field: the Hofheimer Prize for Research, which is awarded by the American Psychiatric Association, and Yale University's Wilbur Lucious Cross Medal. In his most recent book, *The Second Year,* he explains his research on fearful children. He is also the author of *Understanding Children* and co-author of *Child Development and Personality* and *Birth to Maturity.*

Dr. Robert B. McCall advised on the sections of the book discussing IQ testing and genetic influences on intelligence. Currently Professor of Psychology and Director of the Office of Child Development at the University of Pittsburgh, Dr. McCall has conducted extensive research on hereditary and environmental influences on learning and on developmental changes in IQ. In addition to serving on the editorial boards of several psychological journals, he is a contributing editor of *Parents* magazine, where he writes the monthly "About Fathers" column.

Contents

4 Children with Special Needs   78

5 Foundations for Learning   90

The Importance of Nurture

A one-year-old reaches out for a marigold held in her mother's hand, and a learning experience is underway. The child feels the smooth stem of the flower and sniffs its pungent scent. Transfixed by the petals' bold orange color, the little one hears her mother's familiar voice: "Flower. See the pretty flower?" As the young mind gathers these sensory messages, new connections are formed, associations made and memories stored away. Before many months have passed, the dividends of this brief experience and others like it will be evident. The child, seeing another marigold, will turn to her mother and say, "Flower! Pretty flower."

Indeed, to babies and young children, all the world's a classroom and each day is filled with tiny but important lessons. And most of these lessons are taught by the child's first and most influential guides — her parents. While it is true that a child's ability to master life's lessons is determined to a great extent by the mental capacities she is born with *(pages 34-39),* her environment and the people who interact with her also exert powerful influences on her learning ability.

As the following pages explain, there is much you can do as a parent to help your child develop her natural abilities to the fullest — however broad or limited they may be. This is not to suggest that you should begin bombarding her with the three R's at an early age. Rather, at all ages and stages you should give your child such commonsense parental gifts as stimulation, encouragement and freedom to explore. Remember, too, that intellect is only one aspect of a child's overall potential: Brain power must be rounded out by physical, emotional and social well-being if a child is truly to flourish.

Environmental Influences

For the better part of a century, child development studies have revolved around a central question: How much of a child's mental ability is determined by nature — the genes he inherits from his parents — and how much depends on nurture, the shaping influences of the people and things that surround him?

A hundred years ago, people generally assumed that intellectual potential was fixed at birth: A child was destined by nature to be bright or dull, regardless of the effects of his environment or training. Thinking on this point shifted during the early years of the 20th century, when Sigmund Freud, the father of psychoanalysis, first popularized the idea that early childhood experience was critical to an individual's later development. Freud's theories propelled the pendulum toward an emphasis on environment, and scholars began examining the effects of nurture on a child's mental abilities. Was it possible that early intervention, in the form of teaching and other focused attention, could actually increase a child's brain power?

The effects of intervention

Certainly, such techniques had produced spectacular results in some extreme situations. In a number of celebrated cases, researchers noted that children made astonishing intellectual gains when they were taken out of oppressive institutional settings or disadvantaged homes and placed in foster homes where they received the benefits of a normal family life. These results seemed to send a clear message: Nurturing can enhance mental performance.

In later studies using laboratory animals, researchers found evidence suggesting that concentrated training might actually physically increase brain power. One famous experiment divided pairs of twin rats into two groups: Those in the first group were kept together and treated to a life of toys and exercise equipment, learning challenges and rewards for performance, and frequent field trips to explore unfamiliar environments. Their twin brothers, meanwhile, were kept in solitary cages and denied such stimulating experiences. Not only did the favored rats outscore their siblings on problem-solving intelligence tests, the scientists found that the animals had also developed larger, heavier brains as a result of the stimulation they had experienced.

Skeptics are quick to point out, however, that the development of human children cannot be equated with that of rats, and that there is no hard evidence that forced learning in early childhood has any lasting effects. Furthermore, some experts warn that the potential harm outweighs any educational gains children might derive from this hothouse approach to child rearing *(pages 20-22).*

The debate over timing

A related controversy is the timing of a young child's learning experiences. Some psychologists maintain the Freudian view that experiences during the first three years of life have an effect on a youngster's development that can never be undone. Others consider this far too drastic a view and contend that a loving, nurturing environment can produce positive results whenever the child experiences it, overriding earlier negative influences *(box, pages 10-11).* By the same token, they believe, an environment that discourages learning can counteract the effects of earlier positive gains. Both sides point to the decidedly mixed lessons of Project Head Start — perhaps the most significant large-scale effort to apply the potential-boosting theories of the environmentalists into the lives of real children.

Launched in the 1960s, Head Start is a classroom enrichment program designed to provide an educational boost to preschool children from disadvantaged backgrounds. The initial results looked promising: When children from the program first entered school, they performed better than comparable youngsters who had not attended Head Start. But after a year or two, they lost the edge they had gained and once again slipped behind the performance level of classmates from more advantaged circumstances. Many experts concluded that for educational enrichment efforts to be effective in the long term, they must be reinforced by influences in the home environment and the society in which the child is growing up.

How nature and nurture interact

Today, the nature versus nurture pendulum sits squarely in the middle: Heredity and environment both play a critical role in determining a child's ability to learn. In the broadest possible terms, it might be said that heredity sets an upper limit on a child's potential, and environmental experiences determine the extent to which that potential is realized. This is to say, for example, that a child who is born retarded will only develop intellectual abilities up to a certain low level, however encouraging an environment he inhabits; and a child born with a capacity for brilliance will perform as a genius only if she receives the environmental stimulation necessary to develop her natural mental ability.

However, this neat model does nothing to explain how nature and nurture interact. Scientists who are exploring the many ways in which the two forces are intertwined note that there is active interplay between the individual and his environment at every stage of development. Not only does the child develop capabilities in response to his environment, it seems the environment responds to the child's inborn traits as well. One group of studies showed that infants born with pleasant, easy dispositions received better care and more stimulating attention from their parents than did infants with more difficult temperaments. According to this pattern, naturally outgoing children may in effect improve their own learning environments, while children born

Enchanted by the sights and sounds of a passing parade, these two preschoolers are also absorbing a rich array of information about the world they live in. The ideal environment for a young child is one that provides him with a variety of such broadening experiences.

with more fearful or reticent personalities will avoid certain types of interaction that are potential learning experiences.

The shaping force of home

While there continue to be many areas of disagreement among experts where children and learning are concerned, nearly everyone agrees that there's no place like home for molding a child's intellectual development.

Research has time and time again revealed a high correlation between a child's mental development and the family's income and education level. Children of well-educated parents with comfortable incomes tend to have higher IQ scores and perform better in school than children from lower-class families. Perhaps the reason is simple economics. Well-to-do parents have more money to provide their children stimulating play materials and educational experiences. Perhaps the natural tendency of children to absorb the values and motives of the people who have raised them comes into play, as well. Being creatures of imitation, youngsters naturally follow the examples set by their earliest and most influential role models. In this way, parents who respect learning, enjoy cultural pursuits and reward achievement perpetuate their lifestyle and values through their children.

While these traits undeniably correlate with social and economic class, they are obviously not dependent on it as a cause. Society has always produced remarkable individuals from both sides of the tracks. In the end, most authorities believe that the strongest influences on a child's development are a few simple basics that money does not in any way guarantee. These include a moderate level of stimulation, adult caregivers who are affectionate and responsive, regularity and consistency in daily routine, a rich language environment and freedom to experiment and explore.

There is some evidence that hands-on exploration — manipulating

An Expert's View

The Resilient Child

Many parents nowadays tend to be overly anxious about the early development of their children. They seem to share the attitude — widespread among psychologists and scholars — that the experiences of a child's first three years are indelibly imprinted upon his brain and dictate the course of his adolescent and adult life. It is as if they picture the young child's brain as a kind of phonograph disk, recording all experience in permanently fixed grooves.

But I disagree with this view, and I think the inflexible phonograph record is an inappropriate metaphor for the young mind. While there is no question that experience influences an individual from the beginning of his life, I do not believe that the earliest messages written on the brain are the hardest to erase, nor do I believe that the effects of that first experience are necessarily difficult to alter. On the contrary, I see much evidence that children are above all else resilient, equipped with biological and psychological mechanisms that allow them to overcome many kinds of negative early experiences and grow up to enjoy a well-adjusted life.

Instead of the phonograph recording, let's consider another metaphor for early childhood learning: For a moment, imagine a painter who has set up his easel on a riverbank to depict the wooded scene before him. In the early morning hours we stop to admire his work, and we see that he has sketched in a few low shrubs. Returning at the end of the day, we note that the canvas is now filled with a thickly forested scene. The little shrubs are gone, integrated into the mass of taller shrubs, trees and other greenery that makes up the whole. So it is, I believe, with the development of children: The experiences of the first few years are only part of a much larger picture. Early sprouts of knowledge branch out, change shape or become engulfed by later, more complex learning.

We know that as children develop, early behaviors are replaced by more mature ones. For example, many children begin to show fear of strangers and of separation from parents at the age of 10 months; they speak in single-word phrases at 18 months; at three years of age they hold an absolute definition of right and wrong. Obviously, these behaviors are only temporary, and they disappear, like the shrubs in our forest scene, as development proceeds.

Yet in spite of this pattern of ongoing change and renewal throughout early childhood, many parents, pediatricians and psy-

and controlling the objects in the immediate environment — is an important form of stimulation. In one study conducted over the course of several years, researchers noted that children who had enjoyed access to age-appropriate toys, books and records during their first two years scored higher on first-grade achievement tests than children who had not had such play materials. The significant factor was not the sheer number of toys, but rather, having an assortment of playthings geared to a range of developmental skills, such as language or eye-hand coordination.

A wider world Children also need variety in their lives. Even as infants, they should not be confined too closely to the home, for the world beyond the front door offers countless opportunities for learning and for enjoyment. As long as the wider environment is reasonably safe and healthy, its actual nature does not matter, especially to the learning child. A suburban toddler will be as thrilled to splash in the community swimming pool as a city child is to ride on your lap in the subway, or a country child is to pick beans or to putter about in the garden. Youngsters do not all respond the same way to the same experiences, and exposing your little one to a wide range of stimulating sights and adventures will increase his chances of finding something special to him.

Eventually, the big world will offer your growing youngster the opportunities he needs to exercise his independence and develop the confidence essential to continued learning. But first, during these early years, he needs most of all someone to teach him how to interpret the lessons that are pouring in from all sides, to help him understand his fascinating environment, to enable him to learn. Providing that guidance is one of your most important functions and responsibilities as a parent. ∴

chologists cling to traditional Freudian notions of development as a long chain of connected experiences, and to the related belief that an individual is likely to suffer long-lasting damage from early traumatic experiences.

These assumptions are not consistently supported by observation. A child who is apathetic or anxious as a result of a bad family situation will remain so only as long as his environment stays the same. If placed in more positive surroundings, he has a very good chance of developing into a mentally healthy child. Research has demonstrated this time and again. One study, for example, investigated a number of malnourished, orphaned Korean children who were adopted by middle-class American families. Six years after their adoption, they had average IQ scores some 40 points higher than similar orphans who had remained in disadvantaged surroundings.

Many other stories have followed the same pattern: When shifted to a better environment, deprived youngsters show a marked improvement in development, even if they spent their so-called crucial early years in unfortunate circumstances. Indeed, in all my observations, a child's ability to respond positively to a new environment is stronger than the influence of previous hardships.

I am not, by any means, suggesting that you should be unconcerned about your child's early years. Do all you can to enhance his development by giving him your love and attention and a wholesome environment. But do not despair and conclude that it is too late to reverse the damage if your circumstances take a temporary turn for the worse — because of a divorce or death in the family, or anything else that may cause your child to be anxious for a time. These are life's hazards, and your child will learn to adapt. When things improve, he is likely to respond accordingly.

Like the image on the artist's canvas, your child's mind is endowed with a vast capacity for growth and change. Change and growth are, after all, the primary characteristics of living systems — not static permanence. Let us all celebrate that resilience.

— Jerome Kagan, Ph.D.
Professor of Developmental Psychology
Harvard University

A Parent's Role

Perhaps the most important thing you can do to help your child develop her potential is to relax. There is no need to set learning goals and teach her anything in the formal sense, and attempts to push her into mastering new skills before she is ready will only be frustrating for both you and your child. Young children are naturally eager to learn about the world; all that parents really have to do is provide access to a wealth of interesting experiences, some guidance and loving encouragement.

If you relax and enjoy your time with your child, you create an environment of warmth and pleasure in which the learning process can take place almost unnoticed. And should you make a few mistakes along the way, you will have ample opportunity to rectify them: It has been estimated that in a single three-month period during the first year of life, a baby has some 32,000 distinct learning encounters with her parents, each of them an occasion for emotion and information to pass between adult and child.

Elements of the learning process

You will find it easier to relax and be confident about your role if you understand the basic pattern and pace of your child's mental development and how they affect learning ability at various ages *(pages 52-77)*. You should also be aware of some of the emotional needs and forces at work within that framework. Among these are self-esteem, which is practically indispensable to healthy intellectual progress, and a growing child's desire for independence. Your child's curiosity and natural drive to master new skills are also powerful engines for the learning process. Knowledge of these elements enables a parent to provide the kind of environment that enhances their positive effects — an environment that responds to the child, stimulates her imagination and offers a large measure of freedom.

Some development guidelines

Researchers in child development have confirmed many things that wise parents seem always to have known instinctively. One of these is that babies are stimulated by their parents' talking to them even before they can understand what is being said. Studies have shown that mothers who talk to their infants a lot tend to produce more competent children than do mothers who address fewer words and sounds to their babies. Early verbal stimulation has a beneficial influence not only on later skill with the spoken word but on reading ability as well.

But initially, language is not a child's primary learning tool. He learns instead through concrete, sensory experiences. He looks on the world as a place filled with wondrous new things to see, hear, touch, taste and smell. At this stage he loves to use his fingers or mouth to explore shapes and textures, and he should be given plenty of safe objects to experiment with.

One of the biggest rewards for parents who learn some of the basic principles of development is being able to stay in step with their children, neither frustrating them with toys or activities too difficult to master nor boring them with overly simple playthings and stories. But every child is different, and you should not expect your youngster to perform strictly in accord with a calendar of development. Although you can learn the stages of progress from the authorities, you will know the pace at which your own child develops only by close observation of the youngster.

The importance of self-esteem

Nothing is more essential to learning, and particularly to the development of those special intellectual qualities of originality and creativity, than self-esteem. A child must be confident enough to risk failure in order to learn, since most learning is a process of trial and error. And in order to become a truly creative person, a child must be sufficiently confident to risk failure on a large scale — sometimes with an audience.

The first step in helping a child build self-esteem is to pay generous attention to him. This is not to say that you must always drop everything at his call or cater to his every demand. But it does mean that you should frequently take the time to give your little one the kind of eye contact, close-listening and undivided attention that lets him know he is an important person. This tells him that his wants and feelings merit serious consideration, that his thoughts are interesting enough to listen to and hear out to the end. You can begin giving your child this message from the earliest days of infancy, by responding promptly to his cries and taking care of his needs. You are not spoiling him with this kind of attention; you are building his confidence, showing him from the beginning that he carries some weight in the world.

Repeated successes create confidence and an expectation of further success. Take notice and praise your child when he learns to button a shirt, draw a circle — however lopsided — or stack one block atop another. In making him feel good about his efforts, you expose him to the pleasure of success and help him to develop a positive attitude toward learning. Because you tell him he is capable, he will think of himself as capable. When the youngster eventually enters school, his firmly established expectation of success will cause him to view reading or arithmetic as just another challenge of the sort that he has regularly mastered.

Go out of your way to help your child succeed, but be subtle. If he is having trouble pouring a glass of milk, for instance, first ask if you can hold the glass, then move it so that it catches the milk. If your daughter is throwing a softball, try very hard to catch it, even if catching

Paying sensitive attention to what your youngster says, as this mother is doing, is one of the best ways to foster self-esteem and encourage intellectual development. Thoughtful responses to a child's questions and opinions let her know that she is important enough to be taken seriously — and give her the confidence to express her thoughts and feelings fully.

it requires a long reach on your part, and tell the youngster that she made a good throw.

When a child is having difficulty with a problem, however, it is best to let him find the solution whenever possible: He will remember best what he discovers for himself. Advise him, but do not interfere or take over the task yourself unless he asks for help. That way you are showing him that you have confidence in his abilities.

How to use praise

Praise is a potent force for encouraging self-esteem — particularly if you take care to focus the praise on your child's accomplishment, not on her value as a person. Say "You did a wonderful job of putting away your toys. That must make you feel proud," rather than, "You're such a good girl for cleaning your room so well." The latter comment implies that if she does not perform to your standards, you may value her less. Praise should be aimed at enhancing the pleasure a child takes in her achievement.

And avoid incorporating comparisons to others in your praise. It is enough to compliment her for doing something well; she does not need to be told that she did it better than her friend. She should feel special and competent, not necessarily superior. A child whose parents have led her to believe that she is smarter or stronger or better-looking than everyone else will have a difficult time making friends.

Encouraging individuality

Although a feeling that she is better than anyone else does not help a child, you should encourage the youngster's sense of herself as an individual. You can tell the child truthfully that there is no one else on earth exactly like her. Her singular set of genes and experiences has made her a unique and therefore special and valuable human being.

Children who are comfortable with themselves as individuals usually rate high in creativity and are also less likely to give in to group pressures later in life. A child who views herself as unique will probably regard other people the same way and be more appreciative of their special qualities. She also is likely to gain the calmness, emotional maturity and independence she needs to experiment and fully explore the world around her.

Dealing with failure

Do not make a fuss about failure. In fact, however far from perfect your child's effort, you usually can find something to praise about it. If the tower collapses when

To a wide-eyed toddler out for a stroll, as simple a sight as a squirrel in a tree can become an exciting opportunity to learn something new. Parents who themselves show curiosity and interest in exploring their surroundings will prompt similar responses from their children.

he adds the fourth block, say "You did very well building a tower that was three blocks high. Why don't you try four blocks again?" Or if the child becomes frustrated at his inability to draw a picture, encourage him with words to this effect: "Cats are very hard to draw, but I think it's wonderful how you never stop trying until you're satisfied." This will reassure the youngster that his efforts are worthwhile. Children are trusting, and they are likely to believe you if you tell them they are doing well.

There is another side to this trust, however. They will also believe you if you tell them they are slow, clumsy or stupid, giving them self-perceptions that will cripple their efforts to learn. Negative comments reinforce the expectation of failure the same way that praise reinforces the expectation of success.

And remember that in self-esteem, as in all other matters, your child pays more attention to what you do than to what you say. So model the view of yourself that you want your child to have of himself. You may not be able to control what you feel about your own failures and shortcomings, but you can exercise care in what you say about yourself in front of your child and how you react to your triumphs and disappointments.

Becoming independent

It is natural for a human being to want to control herself and her own environment — even if she is a very young human being. When a child is eager to exercise some control and you deny her the chance, you are in a sense telling her that she is not competent to have that responsibility, a message that is damaging to her self-esteem. Seek situations where you can allow your child to practice being in charge. If your three-year-old decides to rearrange the patio furniture, for instance, let her. The youngster can spend an hour happily dragging lawn chairs about, feeling important and in control, and you can put them back in place the next day.

The desire for control is part of a natural childhood drive toward independence. You should not resist this quest; instead, help the child learn how to handle independence when she gets it. The best environment for achieving this is a home with a warm and democratic social atmosphere. The word "democratic" in this sense does not mean that a family vote decides vital issues, or that children are treated the same as adults. It does mean that parents control their children's behavior by example, reason and consultation rather than by rigid authoritarianism.

All households need rules, but you can present them in a manner that makes sense to a child. If she resists going to bed at the regular hour, you might explain that she needs the sleep in order to grow, an explanation that respects her intelligence and appeals to her desire to be bigger. You could also point out gently but straightforwardly that parents need some time on their own; the fact that the world does not, after all, revolve around her is a lesson every child must learn sooner or later.

If reasonable rules and explanations are to be accepted, however, the parents' actions must be consistent with the parents' words. A child will naturally resent having to clean up her room if she sees that your bedroom or kitchen is continually messy. Children have a keen awareness of hypocrisy. If you want your child's respect — which you need if you are going to be of any help to her — avoid saying one thing and doing another.

Handling disagreements and decisions

In any home, people disagree. Independence-seeking children disagree with their parents. Parents themselves do not always see eye to eye. While very serious and personal conflicts that might make a child feel insecure are better resolved between parents in private, it is not necessary or even desirable to conceal from youngsters day-to-day disagreements. They can be turned into educational experiences for your child if you handle them in an open, positive and reasoned manner. Children benefit from learning at an early age that people have conflicting points of view and that they can be resolved by discussion and compromise.

Knowing how to make decisions is an essential ingredient in independence, and learning how to make decisions is one of the greatest benefits a child gets from a so-called democratic home environment. By participating in decision making — even on such everyday matters as what color socks to put on in the morning or whether to eat out at a restaurant or stay at home — a youngster learns to size up situations and apply information to the process of choosing among options. Researchers have found, in fact, that children who live in homes where there is abundant discussion and explanation tend to develop sharper mental skills than those children who are left out of family decision-making processes.

Stimulating curiosity

Even very young infants are curious, constantly reaching out to touch things, peering about themselves, turning to look for the source of a noise. As soon as children can crawl or toddle, they begin to poke into drawers, nose into closets and try to climb onto table tops. And once they can talk, children start asking questions — often unexpected, sometimes hard to answer — and endlessly pursue the answers they get with "Why?"

Some psychologists believe that curiosity is an innate drive, possibly a result of natural selection: Because of curiosity, they suggest, certain prehistoric children may have acquired knowledge that enabled them to survive and breed. In any case, the drive — which is stronger in some youngsters than in others — does appear to help children master their environments. While there is no apparent link between a child's level of curiosity and his intelligence, studies have shown that curious children are more creative and more open to new people, ideas and experiences.

You can do much to promote your child's innately curious nature. An act as simple as holding a newborn lovingly can foster the confidence

Finding the Fun in Learning

In the early years, no lesson is more valuable for a child than simply learning to enjoy learning. Most young children will respond enthusiastically to new challenges if they are properly encouraged; above all, learning should be made exciting and fun. Here are some suggestions on how to provide experiences that are both stimulating and satisfying for your child.

- Let your child develop at his own speed and in his own way. If he wants to try to throw a basketball — even in a haphazard or awkward way — let him try. But if he is simply content to watch an adult do it, let him do that, too.

- Follow the child's lead and let yourself be guided by his interests. If you are telling him about the leaves on a tree but he seems to be more interested in the ants on a log instead, let him study the ants.

- Encourage effort and modest improvement — with smiles, hugs and praise — as much as all-out success. If he is having a little trouble completing a puzzle, spend time commending him for the part of the puzzle that he has managed to do: "You got two pieces in. Good for you!"

- Help your child to learn by letting her discover things for herself. If she is curious and wants to know how plants grow, help her plant some seeds: Caring for the plants and watching them develop will teach her more about biology than having the growth process explained to her.

- Build upon one learning experience with a related one. The parent who helps her child plant seeds, for example, would do well to follow up that lesson with a trip to a nursery where her daughter can see greenhouses full of growing plants.

- Show your child how to do a difficult task, such as buttoning his overalls or zipping his jacket, but do not do it for him. By interfering, you are implying that he is not competent.

Instead, encourage him to challenge himself and to practice.

- Set realistic goals for your child so that he will have a chance to experience success. Before you introduce a drawing activity, select a crayon or marker that he can hold easily, and be sure that he is capable of controlling it.

- Relate learning experiences to your child's overall knowledge. If your daughter notices a frozen puddle of water outside on a winter day, remind her that she has seen ice cubes in the freezer. Help her make the connection between the puddle and the cubes by asking whether it is cold outside and what she thinks the temperature inside the freezer is.

- Turn waiting time into learning time. If you are forced to stand in line at the supermarket or wait at the doctor's office, or if you are caught in some unforeseen situation in which your youngster normally would be bored and restless, ask him to count the other people waiting with you or see how many colors he can identify by looking around him.

- Stimulate your youngster's imagination whenever possible. Start out by showing her a photograph in a magazine and ask her what she thinks the people are doing in it, then have her try to make up a story about them.

- Get your child into the habit of setting reasonable goals for herself. Ask her: "Is there something you see Mommy do that you would like to learn how to do?" If your youngster wants to learn how to decorate a cake, for example, you can help her meet that goal by showing her how to do it and by letting her help out with the activity.

- Watch for cues that your child is becoming bored. If you notice your youngster's attention wandering or see that her concentration is on the wane, you should gracefully end the activity for the time being.

and sense of security she will need later to explore her environment. After she learns to crawl or walk, you should encourage her to investigate her surroundings on her own. And when she begins to talk, be sure to take her questions seriously, even though they may try your patience at times. Children place a special value on questions they themselves pose, and they are very likely to remember the answers, so take care to supply well thought-out replies. You can also teach exploratory behavior by example. Children delight in imitating their parents, so if you are openly curious about how a gadget works, why the sky is blue or what lies over the next hill, your child's curiosity will be stimulated along with yours.

A drive for mastery In addition to responding to his own inborn curiosity, his urge for independence and the parental praise that encourages his self-esteem, a child is motivated to learn by another force that the experts explain simply as an innate drive for mastery over his environment — a striving to become competent. Even after all their other physical and emotional needs have been satisfied, babies demonstrate this drive to take on new challenges and persist until they achieve competence. For an example of this motivating force in action, watch a baby trying to stand in his playpen. At the cost of a great deal of energy, the child will eventually haul himself to his feet, totter precariously and then sit down involuntarily and hard. He repeats the performance again and again until he has learned to stand on his own feet. He will do this without encouragement from a parent and even when no one is watching. The effort is prompted solely by the youngster's drive for mastery.

Success increases a child's drive to succeed; a baby who pulls himself to a standing position will next want to stand without holding on, then walk. The same kind of motivation can spur him to higher and higher levels of intellectual achievement.

Playing and learning

Forces such as curiosity and a desire for mastery get involved in a child's play just as they do in learning to crawl or to stand. A young child does not really differentiate between play and other activities: In fact, playing is his primary vehicle for learning in the early years *(pages 90-137)*, and you will want to provide the best possible environment for him to play in.

A child who is old enough to be let out of sight should have free run of the communal parts of your home, to wander and play in at will unless he is making a mess you cannot tolerate at a given moment. But he also needs a place that is particularly his, matched to his abilities, interests and age. The size of the area is not the most important consideration; it can be a separate playroom or even the corner of a bedroom shared with a sibling. But it is important that the youngster be in charge of the space.

Naturally, the play area should contain nothing dangerous. Floor coverings are important; an ideal play area might offer some carpeted area and some bare floor. Storage should be open, since toys are more accessible on shelves than in chests. Nothing should be kept there except what belongs to the child, so that he is free to experiment and play with everything. And, yes, within his play area let him go ahead and create an untidy clutter; although early on you can certainly begin teaching him to straighten up his things and put them away on a regular basis.

Qualities of an ideal environment

A learning environment, of course, extends far beyond a play area — far beyond any physical boundaries. It includes people and attitudes, ideas and forms of behavior. In order for the youngster to make the most of her natural drives, the learning environment needs to have certain qualities.

One quality of extreme importance is what authorities call "responsivity," although that term seems to mean nothing very different from the plain English word, "responsiveness." A child needs an environment that responds to her behavior. The quicker and more consistent the response, the more rapidly she will learn. Responsiveness is at issue when the young infant cries and is either answered or ignored.

Thus it is a quality that is bound up with the child's needs for self-esteem and control. A responsive environment should not be one that caters to a child's whims or unreasonable demands. The responses can be negative as well as positive, as long as they are clear and consistent. If a child willfully rips apart a favorite book in a fit of anger, for instance, the response from her parent might be: "Oh, that's too bad. You'll miss that book, and we certainly won't be buying another copy of it any time soon." The youngster immediately learns the consequences of her action.

Another key quality is freedom. Behavioral freedom must be bounded by limits that are clearly defined and enforced by the parents: Children feel insecure when there are no limits, and when they sense that their courses of action are totally in their own hands. Within the set limits, a youngster should have complete liberty to explore. Physical confinement of the child should be kept to a minimum. A playpen, for instance, can be a handy place to safely stow a toddler or a crawling baby when you must leave her alone in the room for a few minutes, but it is not a fit environment for a child to spend a whole morning in.

While a child needs limits on her actions, she should know that there are no restraints at all on what she thinks or feels. The sentiments that float unbidden to the surface of the child's mind are not subject to the same judgment of right or wrong that applies to actions, and therefore they must not be censured. As a parent, you should instead encourage the youngster to discuss them. If a child is told that certain kinds of ideas or feelings are bad, she will begin to repress them, thus closing off the gateway to her unconscious mind, which should be a lifelong source of originality and creativity.

Finally, an ideal environment for learning is characterized by another quality, which is very closely related to freedom in thinking and feeling, but difficult to name or describe. This special quality is whatever it takes to stimulate a child's imagination. She needs to learn more than reasoning, decision making or how to process factual information. She also needs to learn how to fantasize. You can encourage this development by reading aloud imaginative books that take wing from reality and by telling her your own stories, which shows her that not all stories come from books, that she can create them, too. Imagination, of course, cannot be forced to deliver on demand. A child must be in the mood for fantasizing; but fortunately, most children above the age of three seem to be in the mood much of the time, which is why they spend so many happy hours at pretend play.

No more than forcing imaginative thought can you force your child to participate in any other learning experience, and you should never try. If you regard the whole learning process the same way your child does — as a continuous, lively and fascinating game — you will both have the time of your lives with no effort at all. ❖

A young child needs plenty of freedom to explore the world on his own: The lessons he discovers for himself often leave a stronger impression than those explained by others. This adventurous boy is conducting his own informal experiment on the function of a trickling garden hose — first feeling its cool wetness, then putting it to his mouth for a drink.

When Parents Push Too Hard

It is perfectly natural for parents to want the best for their child — to be eager to prepare him for life's challenges and help him to shine. These good intentions, however, can be carried to extremes. And when teaching becomes pushing and encouragement turns into command, the unfortunate result may be an anxious, rather than an achieving, youngster.

In recent decades, research studies focusing on the immense learning potential of babies and young children led some psychologists to advocate structured education for preschoolers, toddlers and even infants. Attempting to capitalize on what they saw as a once-in-a-lifetime chance to develop their child's brain power, many parents took up teaching their youngsters with a passion. The result was a phenomenon that came to be called the Superkid movement: One could find flashcards held in front of six-month-old infants, toddlers drilled in spelling and preschoolers driven from tennis lessons to computer classes to tutoring sessions in art appreciation and algebra.

Did these educated youngsters really get a valuable head start in life? Most developmental experts say the answer is no. In fact, many child psychologists are convinced that the educational benefits of such drills are transient, and they fear that the negative emotional lessons last all too long. Youngsters who are coached in the right answer to every question, these experts say, can become afraid to think for themselves. Pressured children often learn to fear failure at an age when they should be constantly testing new ideas. Such children might even come to feel that they are loved for their achievements, not for themselves. Worst of all, every day of pushing robs children of what they need most — their freewheeling hours of childhood exploration.

Presented with flash cards, a clock and an abacus, a toddler is more likely to learn about tastes and textures than numbers. Young children start their education with concrete, sensory impressions and move on to abstract concepts only when they reach the appropriate stage in their development.

Why some parents push

Parents push their children for the best and worst of reasons. Most parents have a genuine desire to give their child every advantage. Many parents see their children as reflections of themselves, representatives of their lives, identities and values. Working parents, mothers particularly, often feel guilty about having to leave their children under another's care; some try to compensate by structuring their youngsters' lives, under the assumption that structured time is quality time.

People who see life as a competition and education as the leading edge may transfer this attitude to their children. After all, the reasoning goes, it's a tough world out there, and a child needs every advantage possible in order to go to the best schools — starting with nursery school — and to land the best jobs. Adults who are proud of their achievements may want their children to follow the same path, while other parents perhaps hope their children will succeed where they have failed.

It appears that many of the so-called super parents push because they believe that by not doing so they are depriving their child of precious opportunities. They have become convinced that they can actually make their children smarter and more talented by accelerating the learning process, reasoning that the younger the child is, the more he can learn in a given period of time. Or perhaps they simply view their young pianist or baby mathematician as proof that they are good parents.

Can nature be rushed? Most of the gimmicks that are designed to build a smarter child, however, simply do not work. Furthermore, the critics point out, it is unnecessary for parents or anyone else to push a child into achievement: When children are ready, they learn to speak and walk, to read and write, and to master any number of other complex tasks with no special training.

Readiness, in fact, is a key factor in early learning. It is well established that children pass through a universal sequence of cognitive stages as they develop the mental skills needed to process information *(pages 52-77)*. Attempts to speed up this natural process have largely been unsuccessful.

Preschool children can indeed be drilled and achieve amazing goals — in the short run. However, several studies have shown that early educational gains such as these actually have little lasting effect. Children who were taught to read very early, for example, were found to have no advantage over later readers, once the two groups had been in school for a few years. In addition, follow-up studies of children who were enrolled in Project Head Start — an educational enrichment program that was launched in the 1960s to serve culturally disadvantaged preschoolers — showed that most of the youngsters in the program lost their comparative edge over the others by the time they reached fourth grade.

While this evidence suggests that it is futile to try speeding up the natural pace of learning, it does not mean that a child's intellectual development is inalterable. If, as most psychologists believe, each child is born with a certain range of natural ability, then an attentive, responsive upbringing can certainly help that potential bloom. Parents who applaud their daughter's tuneful singing, take her to hear concerts in the park and offer her piano lessons when her attention span seems long enough are providing the right kind of encouragement for potential musical talent. Those who drag a child away from backyard mudpies to sit at the keyboard every day are likely to produce only a young music-hater instead.

Why pushing is harmful Not only is pushing a child generally fruitless, it may in fact be harmful. Some parents make the mistake of applying adult standards to their child's time; they see him as engaged in either productive work or unproductive play. By this reasoning, they feel that he will benefit more from a session at the computer than from an imaginary space game with his playmate next door. Nothing could be further from the truth: Their child, if he has the aptitude, may indeed turn out to be a computer whiz, but children also need the important emotional and social education that comes with play — lessons such as learning to share and take turns, to love and settle disagreements and to make their own decisions.

Many experts believe that substituting structured activities for free time may actually be detrimental to the youngster's development. Memorizing numbers and letters teaches mimicry, but it may actively inhibit creativity and curiosity in the process. A youngster beset with tasks and goals could also start to judge himself in terms of success and failure, which could lead to his becoming anxious, withdrawing from taking risks and experimenting, and always following the safe and familiar path. Some psychologists fear that early drilling may even backfire by producing children who are apathetic and difficult to motivate in later schooling.

In extreme cases, children who have been put under severe pressure to achieve have developed ulcers and other classic symptoms associated with adult stress: headaches, abdominal pain and fatigue. More complex psychological consequences are delayed, some doctors believe, and do not become evident until the youngster reaches the adolescent years.

Obviously, a few sessions with spelling cards can be an enjoyable pastime for both parent and child — if he is ready and motivated — and the activity will hardly doom a youngster to ulcers. Nevertheless, parents should be careful to monitor the amount of time spent and the degree of pass or fail emphasis that is placed on enrichment activities for their youngster. They should weigh what the child is giving up against what he gains.

Protecting the child in childhood

What, in fact, are the real interests of the child who is subjected to a regimen of accelerated learning? Is early achievement really going to make the youngster a happier and more fulfilled person? Mothers and fathers who want to give their children a head start on success might ask themselves whether life is really a race and whether success is actually such a valuable prize. Or are they pushing achievement on their children for its own sake?

Developmental experts insist that the carefree, early years of play are essential to the learning process, setting the stage for emotional health as well as intellectual growth. A youngster playing freely does not worry about living up to expectations and standards; he has the opportunity to experiment and benefit from mistakes that cost nothing. The child can feel secure that he is loved regardless of what he accomplishes.

Children accomplish a great deal simply by being children. And they have the rest of their lives for adult pressures and goals. ⁖

Using Television Wisely

Television is such a major presence in the average child's life that it has been compared to having another adult in the house. Young children watch a staggering amount of TV: A Nielsen poll in the mid-1980s put the average at more than 28 hours a week for children aged two to five. This is more time than most preschoolers will spend in a classroom and more than they may even spend talking to their parents or playing with friends.

This statistic is particularly disturbing because television programs and commercials so often convey images that are violent, stereotyped, misleading or simply confusing to a young child. Few parents would hire a baby-sitter who filled their child's mind with stories of murder and monsters, mixed with occasional exhortations to buy the latest expensive toy or breakfast cereal; yet many are content to leave this role to the television set sitting prominently in the family room.

Parents, educators and child psychologists who are concerned about the impact of television on children also find cause for alarm in the sheer passivity of TV viewing: The child absorbs information without making any effort in return. Some pass hour after hour in this silent, inactive fashion — time that could have been better spent participating in active or creative play, whether alone or with other children.

Programs geared to children

The picture is not all negative, however, and with proper guidance TV can be a constructive element in a child's environment. Parents who survey the field of children's programming, looking for shows that are specially geared to the needs of their child *(box, page 25)* will find a number of encouraging choices. There are educational programs that introduce fundamentals such as letters, numbers, shapes and colors, and reinforce other skills children learn in nursery school and day-care settings. Television can also teach positive social values, such as sharing and helping others. One frequently cited study reported that children actually became more helpful, friendly and cooperative after watching well-designed children's shows such as *Mr. Rogers' Neighborhood.*

In recent years, a number of high-quality children's entertainments have also become available on video — among them, cartoon anthologies, instructional packages and dramatizations of children's classics.

Toddlers and preschoolers, of course, do not know which shows are best for them; it is up to parents to screen and select programs and to monitor family viewing habits. Educators also believe that parents should watch programs with their children whenever possible — particularly adult-oriented shows — so they can help interpret the often-baffling images that flicker across the screen.

A child's way of watching

Before the age of four, a child's immature perceptual abilities make it difficult for her to understand the sophisticated conventions of most TV programs. Young children often do not see the distinction between

Young children benefit most from watching television programs when their parents watch with them — to explain away confusing images, point out misleading statements or merely discuss the meaning of what the child is seeing. Television viewing should be a special activity with clear rules and schedules: The set should never be a baby-sitter.

television drama and real life; for them, the action on the screen is really happening, and they are part of it. They also may not grasp subtleties of characterization. Characters tend to be either all good or all bad to young children, and they become confused when heroes and villains do not act according to their notions of good and evil.

Children under the age of four may have trouble following the sequence of events in a television program, as well. For example, a three-year-old may become anxious when she sees a character in distress, just as adults do. Unlike adults, however, the child is not relieved when the hero rides to the rescue in the next scene. For a young child, each scene is a separate incident, unrelated to the one before. She might not even recognize the characters from the previous scene. And events may pass by too quickly for her to comprehend, leaving her jittery and confused; even acclaimed programs such as *Sesame Street* have been criticized for providing too much information at too fast a clip.

Television can also distort reality in ways that confuse and even frighten children. Time bends to suit the needs of a half-hour or hour-long programming format. On television, a house can be built in a few minutes, a child can grow to adulthood over a commercial break and a conversation frozen in midsentence in one scene will continue from that point minutes later, interrupted by a totally unrelated dramatic scene, a commercial or perhaps a paid political announcement.

Camera trickery — and the accompanying effects on perspective — may baffle children as it bedazzles them. A fantasy character who stands just a few inches tall in one scene may be as big as a barn in the next. Action may lapse into slow motion or merge into a dream sequence. Adults are not confused; but there is nothing in the experience of young children to tell them that this does not happen in real life.

Violence and role models

No element of TV has been more thoroughly debated and studied than dramatized violence. One statistician estimated that the average child sees more than 1,000 people killed on TV each year; countless more are bashed and maimed. What does all this mayhem teach a child?

Controversy abounds on this question. Although a few experts say that TV violence does children no serious harm, several studies have suggested that watching an excessive amount of it may have a number of ill effects — including making a child fearful for his own safety, desensitizing him to violence and encouraging aggression toward others.

The children being observed did not generally imitate specific acts of violence they saw on television, but those who watched four or more hours of TV a day had fewer inhibitions against violence and behaved more aggressively toward other children. One significant study of young adult criminals concluded that the televised violence they watched as children contributed to the violence they later displayed toward their victims. However, a child's temperament seems to be an important factor: those who have a low threshold for aggression feel the influence most, while calm, stable children are the least affected.

Educational experts point out that the messages conveyed by violent

Selecting Programs for Your Child

In selecting television programs and videocassettes for your toddler or preschooler, you will want to accentuate the positive — those entertainments that are simple, gentle and imaginative — and eliminate the negative, which includes any show that may frighten, confuse or encourage aggressive or dangerous behavior. The following guidelines, based on the advice of child psychologists, will help you choose appropriate fare.

- Pick shows with a unifying adult figure who expresses interest in and concern for the child. This will convey a message of stability and authority.

- Ask yourself if the show encourages imaginative play. Does it have characters that your child will want to imitate later? Such play can turn television viewing into an active experience.

- Avoid programs with a cynical or negative slant. Young children can best handle warm, positive scenes, and they may appreciate sweetness that seems too sugary to adults.

- Gauge the material's entertainment value: Does it have some humor? Will it introduce your youngster to new sights and experiences?

- Be on the lookout for shows that are related to your child's interests. If your child is fascinated by animals, for example — as many children are — watch the listings for the fine animal documentaries that TV occasionally offers.

- Be sure the programs your child watches draw a clear line between fantasy and reality. Ideally, an adult narrator or character should introduce a fantasy show as such.

- Do not watch shows in which parents, animals or children are threatened or harmed. Similarly, steer your youngster away from violent cartoons. Young children identify all too closely with these situations.

- Look for programs that move slowly. Rapid-fire action can leave preschoolers confused and disoriented.

- Stay away from spooky shows involving monsters or the supernatural. Remember that a child may not be able to distinguish between real life and TV.

- Avoid programs that glorify dangerous athletic activity or stunts; your child may want to imitate them. If you do see such actions while watching with your youngster, explain that they are performed by specially trained actors or produced by camera tricks.

---

shows are as disturbing as the violence itself. The consequences of violent acts are rarely seen; someone badly beaten in one incident may be walking around unscathed in the next scene. And violent programs tend to glorify both the heroes who solve their problems with fists or guns and the villains who flout authority and get away with it.

In addition to violence, television shows have traditionally carried a heavy load of social stereotyping. While this has changed in recent years, distorted sexual and racial characterizations are still abundantly present in the reruns of old situation comedies that young children often watch. Shows portraying women as household drones or empty-headed sex objects, men as insensitive dupes, and the entire world as white and middle class do not help a child to understand real life.

The hard sell Scrutiny of these and other problems has led to improved family comedy programs over the years, but television advertising has lagged behind, particularly in observing the rules of fair play. As with advertisements for adult products, children's commercials attempt to create a need where none existed before. But young children are far less able than grownups to evaluate what they are being shown on TV. Toys often loom larger than life on the television screen, pictured against a fantasy landscape, their child owner surrounded by admiring friends. When the small, disassembled, batteries- and friends-not-included product arrives at the house, it can be a considerable disappointment.

Some children's programs, particularly in the Saturday morning time slots, are thinly disguised vehicles for selling new products, their cartoon characters deliberately creating a confusion between television fantasy and toy-store reality. Parents can help children deal with the pressures of TV advertising by watching commercials with them, pointing out the exaggerations.

Establishing guidelines early on Because of television's many drawbacks, a few child psychologists have gone so far as to say that it would be best for children not to watch it at all until they have learned to read. However, even these idealists acknowledge that this is unlikely in the majority of households. Most experts feel it is enough for parents to supervise their children's TV watching closely, establishing clear rules and routines very early — even before the child really becomes interested in television.

A child usually becomes aware of the bright colors, sounds and motions on the screen between 12 and 18 months of age, but at this stage television viewing should not be a regular part of her life. You may want to begin introducing your toddler to special programs when she is around two, keeping in mind that her attention span is likely to be very short. At this age, a simple, gently paced show such as *Mr. Rogers' Neighborhood* is best. Keeping to a clearly defined schedule — watching the same show at the same time each day — helps to establish TV watching as a special activity, rather than a random way to fill up time.

By the age of three or three and a half, your child will probably be eager to watch a broader selection of programs. Faster-paced chldren's fare such as *Sesame Street* and some cartoons that you have screened and selected are appropriate to add now to the shows previously introduced. You should be aware that three- and four-year-olds have more highly developed reactions and are more likely to be frightened by what they see on television. Ironically, many psychologists warn against allowing children to watch cartoons at this stage, pointing out that preschoolers can be unnerved by the way cartoon characters are blown up, run over and otherwise maimed and dismembered. It is also easy to misread the reactions of a child at this age; your daughter may seem to be entranced by Big Bird on *Sesame Street,* but she may actually be intimidated by the character's exaggerated size and motions.

At about the age of five or so, children can be introduced to more sophisticated programs that will expand their horizons and stimulate creativity — shows that retell legends and myths, realistic animal stories and programs on dance or puppetry, as well as carefully selected family comedies, animated features and, yes, the ubiquitous cartoon series.

Research into the effects of television on children indicates that children are more positively influenced by shows they watch and discuss with their parents than those they watch alone. You should make a point, therefore, to watch television with your child whenever possible, encouraging her to talk about interesting parts and explaining points that are hard for her to understand.

Here too, as in every other area, children are influenced by their parents' behavior: If you wish to limit your child's TV viewing, you will probably have to limit your own. And to help establish a deliberate, pick-and-choose attitude toward television viewing, be sure to turn the set off when no one is watching it ∴

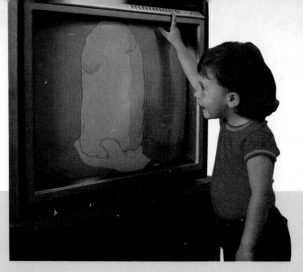

The Mixed Blessings of TV

Is television good or bad for children? Experts continue to debate that question. Here, some parents reveal their own concerns — and satisfactions — with the effects of TV watching on their toddlers and preschoolers.

66 We realized how impressionable our 20-month-old son, David, was after he saw a cartoon in which a duck fell into a vat of boiling liquid. Suddenly he was terrified of taking a bath. Finally we told him that we got rid of the tape of that cartoon and he didn't have to worry about it any more, and slowly we introduced him to the water again. From that time on, we tried to watch TV with him so we could explain things he was too young to understand. **99**

66 It worried me when I noticed that my son was imitating Superman and was getting just a little too brave, jumping from the sofa or high steps. I could just imagine him putting on a towel for a cape and springing out of a window. I carefully pointed out to him that Superman was a fantasy character and that no real person could ever fly like that. **99**

66 I was bothered by my young children's TV-watching habits — to see them crouched immobile in front of the set when I felt they could be doing something else, such as playing outside, jumping around, anything besides just sitting there. We mainly let them watch it just before suppertime, thinking it would keep peace in the household. Then one day, like an act of God, there was a little 'poof' on the screen and no more picture — no more TV! I didn't get it fixed right away, and within a week I realized things were better around the house without it. In retrospect, it hadn't even kept the peace before supper. The kids wound up entertaining themselves in their own way — reading, playing outdoors, making things. We've never had TV again in our home. **99**

66 Cartoons had a mesmerizing effect on Jared. It was difficult to pull him away from them. We would say, 'You can watch one cartoon,' and at the end of that one he would beg to watch more. He'd sit there four hours straight if he was allowed. It worried us so much we decided he could not watch any cartoons at home. He protested at first, but eventually he accepted it. **99**

66 Saturday morning is our opportunity to sleep late, so we let our kids get up and turn on the TV set themselves. I know they are in the house and safe, so I feel TV is a good baby-sitter on weekend mornings. It also helps me get my housework done to let them watch on weekday mornings — though I'd never let them watch it all day. **99**

66 I think it confuses children when they see adult shows, because they don't understand the vocabulary or the issues. After our daughter watched a detective show about blackmail she asked me, 'Why don't we get any black mail? All our letters come in white envelopes.' It made me wonder what other misconceptions she might have formed. **99**

66 It bothers me that the networks air commercials for R-rated horror films during prime time right before children's shows. My two-year-old has been frightened repeatedly by these things. I try to distract him, but the dramatic music draws him like a magnet. I also tried turning the TV off during these commercials, but that just seemed to pique his curiosity. **99**

66 After I've been on my feet all day at work, I love to come home and relax watching TV with my four-year-old. We cuddle and talk about the shows we're watching. I let her fall asleep on the couch, then I put her to bed. **99**

66 We have been very hesitant in encouraging TV watching for our 15-month-old. As a result, she cannot count, doesn't know what a letter is and only knows Big Bird as the stuffed animal in her crib. However, she already seems to have a vivid imagination, she loves looking at books, and she plays beautifully by herself. We simply don't want our TV to be a baby-sitter. As she grows older, though, we plan to gradually introduce her to some TV, because we believe that to be too rigid on this issue might just lead to fanatic TV watching later. **99**

66 Considering all the negative things you hear about TV and young children, I'm kind of ashamed to think how I used to prop Rosie up in her infant seat and let her watch *Sesame Street* before she could even crawl. But she seemed to love it, watching those letters and numbers zing around the screen. I never realized the effect it was having until I took her to the pediatrician for her 18-month-old checkup and she toddled around behind the nurse's desk and started reading the alphabet letters off the file folders! By three, she was reading the newspaper — totally self-taught. It pleased me in a way, but I think there's something a little scary about this power of TV. **99**

A Child's-Eye View

Once your child begins to master language, it may seem impossible to stop him from talking. He chatters on endlessly — not only to you, but to toys, stuffed animals and imaginary playmates. As you listen to what he has to say, it quickly becomes apparent that his way of looking at the world is quite different from that of a grownup. His way is naive, charming and often wildly imaginative. It includes beliefs that experience and growing knowledge will soon modify, but it also is rich with perceptions that older folk may miss. An understanding of this child's-eye view of reality will help greatly as you encourage your youngster's natural curiosity and creativity and assist him in developing his mental and physical skills.

Many of the preschooler's ideas are similar to those held by our primitive ancestors — young and old alike. For example, the two- or three-year-old talks to inanimate objects as though they were alive. In his mind they are. He believes in magic and the supernatural, and he takes everything he sees or hears quite literally — a habit that leads to fanciful explanations for whatever he does not understand.

Above all, he grasps the world — people, pets, even natural phenomena — from his own perspective only. A child of two, for instance, covers up his eyes and says to his mother, "Now you can't see me." He assumes that things he did — or failed to do — explain other, unrelated, events. He might say, "I haven't had my nap, so it isn't afternoon."

To be sure, this ingenuous perception of the world is not unique to childhood; amusing remnants of ancient thought processes survive among sophisticated adults. Some talk lovingly or angrily to their houseplants and even to their cars, while others, carrying umbrellas on a cloudy day, explain, "It's to prevent rain." But most adults do these things without believing in their efficacy. Grownups have already acquired more rational concepts of everyday experience — of logic, cause and effect, time, size, quantity, distance and sequence. This growth in knowledge comes rapidly in the early years of life, as a child learns of the world firsthand *(pages 52-77)*.

How rapidly the child's-eye view starts to mature is indicated by changes in a youngster's understanding of money. Given the choice of several pennies or a dime, most three-year-olds focus on the size or number of the coins and choose the pennies, assuming that because they are larger and there are more of them, they are worth more. But by the age of five or six, children begin to learn that coins have different values.

Your own child's fantastic stories and delightfully twisted explanations of the world around him may be like those illustrated here and on the following pages. You may wonder, "How does he come up with these things?" The answer is simple: It is part of growing up.

A world where objects have feelings

A conversation with a tree — or any other inanimate object — seems perfectly natural to most three-year-olds. After all, the tree has limbs that resemble arms and move in the wind; so it must be alive, like a person. And then, it must also have thoughts and feelings, just as people do. A young child who trips over a chair may say, "Sorry, chair, I didn't mean to hurt you." He wonders whether the grass hurts when his daddy mows the lawn or whether the sun is sad when it rains. And he thinks that the wind is alive because it blows.

Bending the laws of physics

If a man's voice is coming out of a radio, a preschooler assumes there is a real man speaking inside the radio. Never mind that she knows a man is too big to fit inside a radio: In the magical world of childhood, people shrink and grow at will. With no understanding of the complex physical principles underlying such a feat, the youngster simply accepts the idea — just as many young children unblinkingly accept the notion of Santa Claus coming down the chimney. It is not until they reach school age that children begin to distinguish between what is physically possible and impossible. Thus, an older child begins to question how Santa could fit down a chimney and visit every child in the world in just one night.

A belief in the magic of rituals

A young child takes to heart such nursery rhymes as "Rain, Rain Go Away." Merging reality and fantasy, she believes in the magical power of rituals and of her own thoughts and actions to make things happen. No doubt it is comforting for a young child to feel that she can exert some control over her environment. Most preschoolers adore Maurice Sendak's book, Where the Wild Things Are, in which Max tames the wild creatures "with the magic trick of staring into all their yellow eyes without blinking once." But personal power can also be intimidating. Many a youngster, for instance, fears that stepping on a crack really could break her mother's back.

Lopsided logic

What do all grownups have in common in the eyes of a three-year-old? They are tall. So the child concludes that if she climbs on a stool to make herself tall, she will be grown-up. This delightfully lopsided style of reasoning and generalizing during the preschool years is a result of the child's focusing on just one aspect of an issue at a time. Thus, noticing only that grownups are tall leads to the notion that height must determine age: "If I'm tall, I must be old." In Lewis Carroll's Alice's Adventures in Wonderland, the bewildered heroine reached the same conclusion when she grew very tall after sampling a bottle of liquid in the White Rabbit's house: "There ought to be a book written about me," said Alice, "that there ought! And when I grow up I'll write one — but I'm grown up now."

Confusing cause and effect

If the calendar says it is spring, a late March snow is not going to stop a four-year-old from going outdoors to play baseball. Young children believe that the calendar controls the seasons, regardless of the weather. Lacking a clear concept of cause-and-effect relationships, preschoolers draw many odd conclusions of this sort about the way things happen. They especially tend to link simultaneous occurrences — believing, for example, that honking the horn makes the car go, or that night falls because they go to sleep.

Seeing is believing

Most three-year-olds are transfixed with delight at the sight of a clown or of an actor decked out in the costume of a favorite cartoon character. In their eyes, these are not just people wearing funny costumes and make-up. The costumes have transformed them into the friendly, colorful characters they appear to be. They are what they look like, for children at this age do not distinguish between real and make-believe. For the same reason, a child may be genuinely terrified by a person wearing a grotesque costume or scary mask: He believes the figure is as sinister as its appearance suggests.

A self-centered universe

Because a young child understands life from her own point of view only, she sees herself dwelling at the center of a world created for her benefit. If she notices the sun high in the sky when she leaves home, for example, and she sees it there still when she reaches her destination, she assumes that the sun has followed her. The egocentric preschooler believes that family life, too, revolves around her and her concerns. Thus when her mother is distracted by a headache or a cold, the child may well be oblivious to her mother's feelings and wonder instead, "Why doesn't Mommy want to play with me today? I must have done something to make her angry."

Taking language literally

Until they master adult idioms, children often misinterpret language in amusing ways. If you tell a young child, "Daddy will be home late because he's tied up at work," the youngster is likely to picture his father bound to a chair with ropes. He may assume that the North Pole is a long stick, and he may expect to find "signs of spring" like billboards along the highway.

The reality of dreams

With her penchant for making up explanations for things she cannot understand, a preschooler may say that dreams "come from under my pillow." But however they arrive, her dream images seem as real as events that occur during waking hours. Children of this age often get dream life and real life mixed up. This is why it is sometimes difficult to calm a child after she has had a nightmare. It also explains why she may insist she did something that no one else can recall. "Don't you remember the time we went to Grandma's and I slept in a tent?" an exasperated child asks her baffled parents. Of course they cannot remember; it happened in her dream.

Make-believe friends

Her mother has heard nothing, but three-year-old Nancy insists there was a knock at the door. When they open it, her mother sees no one, but Nancy welcomes an invisible friend she calls Nan-Nan. "You can't tell Nan-Nan anything," warns Nancy. "She only listens to me." Such imaginary playmates enrich the lives of many three-year-olds. Often, the invented character is a mirror image of the child herself — indicated by similarities in names — who is conjured up to fulfill the role of confidant, companion, and protector in scary situations.

Solutions to nature's mysteries

If you ask a child where rain comes from, he might answer that the giant who lives up in the clouds sometimes forgets to turn his faucet off and water overflows onto the ground. Like the earth's ancient inhabitants, young children cannot possibly be expected to comprehend the immense workings of nature. They usually attribute such mysteries as weather and ocean waves and stars to human actions or to witches, fairies or other supernatural creatures that resemble humans.

A scrambled sense of time

The vacation-packed car is barely out of the driveway before the three-year-old begins asking, "Are we there yet?" No, her parents tell her, it is an hour's drive to the beach. Within five minutes she has asked the question several more times. Most children of this age have no concept of such time units as a minute, hour or week, and therefore they lack a mental measure of time's passage. Preschoolers may also equate distance with time: A destination an hour away by airplane seems closer than one three hours away by car.

33

2 Nature's Contribution

Like all identical twins, the two bright-eyed boys pictured at right have inherited precisely the same set of genes, half from their mother and half from their father. And if we could peer through those eyes into the minds beyond, we would most likely find that their mental abilities are strikingly similar — closer than the mental match existing between themselves and their mother, their father or any other siblings in the family.

Since scholars cannot see a blueprint of the human mind in their search for the origins of human intelligence, they have focused their research efforts on test scores for groups or pairs of individuals who share close versus distant genetic relationships. And to date, some of the more persuasive evidence to support the argument for heredity as the prime shaper of intelligence has come from studies of identical and fraternal twins in the U.S. and Western Europe. The scores for identical twins, who share all of their genes, correlate more closely than scores of any other kinship group — 86 percent — a dramatic leap over the 55 percent mental similarity for fraternal twins who share, on average, half their genes.

But these figures are only one small step in the quest for a fuller understanding of human intelligence. Most authorities agree that children inherit a substantial portion of their basic mental potential from their parents, a potential that must then be developed through various learning experiences. But the dividing line between these dual aspects of mental ability — heredity and environment — is anything but clear.

The following pages describe the ongoing efforts of researchers to explore the questions that remain unresolved concerning the true nature of intellectual ability and how it can best be measured. In what complex ways do inborn ability and experience play off one another? And what are the ultimate human limits?

The Meaning of Intelligence

Since Plato's time, scholars have been debating the slippery subject of human intelligence, struggling to pinpoint its precise nature. A clear-cut definition, however, continues to elude us. As with other such issues, there seems to be more agreement about what intelligence is not than about what it is. Experts concur that it is not a physical entity or organ. Although intelligence is clearly centered in the brain, the mere possession of large amounts of cerebral gray matter does not ensure a high intelligence level. Nor can intelligence simply be equated with IQ — the intelligence quotient that represents a score on the most widely used standardized tests of mental ability. Some people do not score well on IQ tests but are clearly bright in other ways.

In the broader sense, intelligence is often looked upon as a set of behaviors related to the individual's ability to understand and cope with the challenges of life — whatever those challenges may be. As such, it is a relative concept that can incorporate any number of very different abilities or skills — from solving complex equations or building a piece of furniture to playing a difficult piano concerto or finding a safe pathway out of the wilderness.

Cultural considerations

Our particular definition of intelligence reflects our own culture and history. The behaviors we describe as intelligent are tailored to life in a modern, scientific and highly urbanized culture. The demands of this type of culture place a high value on skills such as fluency with language, and the ability to manipulate numbers and to reason in a logical fashion. We value thinking skills such as the facility to see relationships among diverse things, to solve problems in a systematic fashion, to learn from experience and to adapt to changing environments or circumstances. And we place a premium on speediness and flexibility in dealing with such challenges.

In ancient societies values were different, and intelligence was sometimes very narrowly defined by such criteria as knowledge of religious law or skill in public oratory. In rural subsistence cultures, on the other hand, intelligence encompassed a much larger physical component, incorporating endurance, coordination and hunting skills that enabled community members to raise, gather or capture food. Even in the modern world, concepts of intelligence may vary somewhat from one culture to another.

The popular view of intelligence was radically altered by a watershed event that took place in Paris in 1905 — the first use of Alfred Binet's intelligence test to assess children's academic potential in the overcrowded French schools of the day. Although Binet never intended the test as anything more than a means of predicting success in school, IQ score became synonymous with intelligence over the years. And in fact, that original testing pro-

A three-year-old's mastery of a jigsaw puzzle requires a grasp of spatial relationships and problem-solving skills — just two of the many different kinds of mental ability that contribute to the composite quality that is known as intelligence.

cedure still underlies most of the tests of general mental ability in use today *(pages 40-46).*

The sum versus the parts

IQ scores have also served as convenient yardsticks for scholars in the study of various aspects of intelligence. One major avenue of research has focused on the question of its qualitative nature — whether humans are endowed with a single, central intelligence factor or many different mental abilities that operate independently of each other.

During the first half of the 20th century, psychologists who studied the results of tests of different mental abilities that were administered to the same subjects made what they thought to be a striking discovery: No matter which test a youngster took, his relative score was very similar from one test to another. Since each test apparently rated a different set of particular mental abilities, the psychologists concluded that intelligence is unitary in nature and that some general intelligence factor, which they labeled *g,* underlies all the different mental skills.

This notion of a general mental ability was later challenged by other scholars who argued that intelligence is merely the sum of its parts — a composite of separate abilities such as word usage, creativity and numerical skills. One professional claimed to have identified as many as 120 different such categories of ability. Proponents of the composite theory observed that children with identical IQ scores often scored quite differently on the subtests, which, when combined, make up the overall IQ score. Thus, they concluded, two children with exactly the same IQ may possess rather different patterns of specific intellectual capabilities.

While both sides of this long-running dispute made persuasive points, neither the older theory of a single, unitary intelligence nor the newer theory of many independent abilities was entirely satisfactory. In recent years, many psychologists have been leaning toward a theory of intelligence that combines the two views: They suggest that mental ability is organized in hierarchical fashion, incorporating both a general intelligence factor and descending levels of specific abilities. The overall factor can be compared to general athletic ability: Someone who excels at baseball or track and field, for example, is generally skilled in many sports. Likewise, a youngster who is adept at one mental task tends to perform well in other areas, too. But each person's general ability leaves room for distinctly different patterns of subordinate skills. Using the same example, you might say that while a 250-pound football star may perform well in shot-put, it is unlikely that he will star in the high jump or have a fast finishing time in the marathon. Similarly, a child who is generally bright may be better at reading and telling stories than at programming a computer or writing music.

The role of heredity

While experts have argued long and hard over the relative influences of native versus acquired ability where intellect is concerned *(pages 8-11)*, most have accepted the idea that some portion of a child's intellectual make-up is inherited. But how much? We can observe, informally, that intelligent parents tend to produce bright children; but researchers have not yet been able to devise the appropriate scientific tools to measure exactly how genetic influence — the passing on of genes from parents to child — works in determining the mental and physical capabilities of individuals.

Geneticists agree that there is no single master gene responsible for intelligence, and it even seems unlikely that a person's particular skills and abilities are directly linked to particular genes. Instead, researchers believe that hundreds of genes, which are as yet unidentified, may be involved in transmitting the many traits that are associated with intelligence.

Moreover, those genes may appear in a wide variety of combinations. A child inherits half of his genes from his mother and half from his father, in a process that may be roughly compared to rolling a pair of dice: The fact that the same pair of dice may come up showing two sixes one time, snake eyes another time and a four and a five the next can help us to understand why brothers and sisters display wide variations in individual mental skills, or why a set of parents with average intelligence may occasionally produce a highly gifted child or a child with below-average intelligence.

Studies of identical twins

Lacking a full understanding of the biochemistry of gene action, scientists have largely looked to an approach called population genetics to discover traits that seem to be passed on from parents to children — including those traits associated with intelligence. Specifically, by comparing and contrasting the IQ scores of many pairs of individuals with differing degrees of kinship to each other, scientists have estimated how much of the overall differences between them is attributable to hereditary, as opposed to environmental, influences.

When intelligence is studied in this broad-brush fashion, evidence of a substantial genetic contribution to intelligence emerges. The relative IQ scores of parents and children, and of brothers and sisters, are more similar than those of genetically unrelated people — even adopted children raised in the same house, for example. And the closer the genetic relationship, the greater the relative similarity. Identical twins, who were produced by a single fertilized egg and consequently have exactly the same genetic make-up, are more similar in IQ than are fraternal twins, who share approximately half of the same genes.

The results of studies of twins appear to provide strong support for the belief that intelligence runs in families for genetic reasons. Even so, sorting out the separate contributions of heredity and environment is very difficult. Critics of the genetic approach point out that, in addition to sharing the same genes, twins who are raised together presumably share nearly identical environments and are subjected to many of the same shaping influences in the home. It is true that in most cases where researchers have been able to study identical twins who were raised in separate environments, their IQ scores are not as close as those of twins raised together.

How genes and environments interact

Heredity appears to play a dominant role in specific, specialized activities such as mathematical skill or musical talent. But here, too, experience is an important shaping force. For example, no amount of parental encouragement and professional training can turn an average child into a musical genius if he does not have the inborn potential to excel. On the other hand, a child who is born with the magic combination of genes to make him musically gifted is unlikely to reach his full potential without encouragement, training, practice and motivation.

Another subtle way environment interacts with inborn ability is the process some scholars refer to as "niche-picking": It seems that children will gravitate toward those pursuits they can perform best, by sampling various activities and situations until they find a comfortable niche. On finding their particular niche, whether it may be an athletic, verbal or artistic skill, the child is rewarded with stimulation, entertainment and the psychological benefits of achievement. These environmental responses serve to reinforce the child's original choice, encouraging further development of those skills.

As a parent, you shape your child's environment as well as his genes. For example, children whose parents read to them are known to perform better in school than those whose parents do not. But parents who like to read to their children usually like to read for their own enjoyment as well. Those parents, then, may pass along both a genetic disposition toward reading and an environment in which reading is encouraged and reinforced.

The limits of intelligence

In recent years, the compelling question has been raised of just how far human intellectual capacities can be expanded. Even though heredity may be a major factor in an individual's mental ability, it is possible that environmental influences could alter the picture over time. Psychologists point to height, a highly hereditary trait, as an example. Like intelligence, height clearly runs in families; if you are tall, your children are likely to be tall. But while this trait is dominated by genetic influences, the average height of children in this country has steadily increased over the last half-century. Changes such as this are plainly linked to improvements in the environment, including better nutrition and better health care.

In the same fashion, some experts believe, environmental influences constantly interact with the inborn components of intelligence — and may well make it possible for people to rise above genetic constraints in as yet undiscovered ways.

But most authorities agree that there are no firm answers to such questions about the ultimate limits of intelligence. The potential of the human mind, they insist, is simply unknown. ∴

Testing Mental Ability

Few topics can stir up parental emotions as readily as the subject of testing children's intelligence. Although IQ tests have been demystified in recent years — and, to some extent, deemphasized — the fact remains that most children are routinely given tests of mental ability soon after they enter school. And the results of those tests can affect the course of a child's school career in both direct and subtle ways.

The history of the IQ test

The most widely used intelligence tests today are essentially adaptations of a turn-of-the-century examination that was not intended to measure general intelligence in the first place. When the French psychologist Alfred Binet developed the initial IQ test in Paris in 1905, he did so for the purpose of distinguishing average pupils from slow learners in overcrowded classes, to help the education ministry identify those who were unlikely to succeed in regular school. As such, his test was designed to assess those skills that children needed to perform well in a general classroom situation; measuring intelligence in a broader sense was not his aim. However, Binet's test was found to be so accurate at predicting school success — and eventually at predicting success at a variety of other tasks — that it came to be used as a gauge of general intelligence.

After several new versions were introduced by Binet, the test was adapted for use in America by researchers at Stanford University, yielding a version called the Stanford-Binet Intelligence Scale. Various other teams later developed similar tests tailored for adults, school-age children and preschoolers.

But despite modifications and innovations over the years, the modern tests based on Binet's model serve the same function now that his did then — as an effective predictor of academic success. A child's IQ scores correlate highly with her current academic performance and, to a lesser extent, predict future scholastic achievement.

Why are children tested?

There is generally no reason for a child to be given an IQ test before she enters school. Before the age of three or so, developmental processes show wide normal variations that may or may not be related to later intellectual ability. For this reason, early intelligence tests are not considered a reliable predictor of a child's eventual academic success. An IQ test might be given along with other diagnostic tests, however, to a preschooler who is experiencing developmental or learning problems or emotional difficulties.

Once your child enters school, he will almost certainly be given one or more group tests of aptitude and achievement. Ideally, these tests serve as tools to help educators identify children who might benefit from special attention, including slow learners who need remedial aid and underachievers who have high IQs but need special assistance to cope with emotional, motivational or learning problems that are hindering their achievement. The IQ test has also become the major means of entry into special programs for gifted children in the public schools *(pages 47-51).*

Although the distinction between IQ and intelligence is blurred in the popular mind, it is important for parents to understand that an IQ test cannot measure intelligence as, say, a scale can measure weight: If your child weighs 30 pounds, she is 10 pounds heavier than a 20-pound child. But if she scores 130 on an IQ test, that does not make her 10 units smarter than the child who scores 120. The most reliable information you can get from this number is that your child's chances of doing well in school are substantially better than average.

How preschoolers are tested

Intelligence tests for young children cover a number of categories, including vocabulary, word usage, memory, reasoning, conceptual thinking and a range of numerical, motor and mechanical abilities. For children too young to take written tests, the examination is given orally in a one-on-one session with a tester. Some of the test items are verbal — the child answers questions put to her by an examiner — and other items require the child to perform a mental task using blocks, drawing materials, puzzles or other objects. In the category of visual-motor skills, for example, a three-year-old might be asked to copy a drawing of a circle; a five-year-old might be given the more advanced challenge of copying a drawing of a square.

By the age of five, the average child can define vocabulary words such as "hat" and "stove," can detect similarities when asked a question such as, "In what way are a crayon and a pencil alike?" and can answer a simple reasoning question such as, "Why do we wear shoes?"

The Distribution of Normal IQ Scores

The stair-step chart at right shows how the distribution of IQ scores falls when a large sample of normal children of the same age is tested using the Stanford-Binet Intelligence Scale. The exact average is reflected in a score of 100. Average scores are established for each chronological age group by giving the test to a large number of children, then determining what score represents the average; the score of an individual child indicates how far above or below the average he scores.

The child pictured reading midway up the stairs is among the 46 percent of the total test group who score between 90 and 109 — the range designated as average. This means that he can correctly complete most of the items in the test that the average child his age can do. A child will score higher than 100 if he can answer questions that usually only older children can manage; a child who cannot accomplish the tasks typical of his age group will score lower than 100. IQ test results for a large sample of normal people will generally fall into what is known as a normal or bell-shaped pattern, with most of the test-takers — about 80 percent — scoring within the low average to high average IQ range between 80 and 120. Only 3 percent score below 70, while a scant 1 percent achieve the very superior category with IQs topping 140.

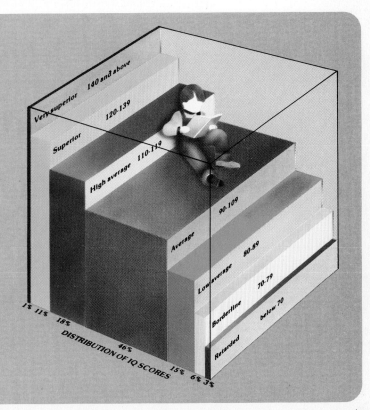

As part of the IQ test she is taking, the five-year-old pictured above must complete a three-piece cardboard puzzle within 30 seconds, by the examiner's stopwatch. If she does not complete the puzzle in time, the examiner will still praise her effort and may show her how to finish.

All tests have timed sections that measure the rate at which a child solves problems. The rationale for this is that nearly every youngster has experience in some basic tasks such as simple arithmetic, but that children differ in the facility with which they are able to solve similar problems.

IQ tests usually measure the quantity of past learning, as well, by determining the relative rarity of information an individual possesses. A child who has learned a great deal will have all of the information that most children have learned, plus some pieces of information that only a few other children know. For example, most five-year-olds would know what the word "flower" means, but only a few would know the word "cactus."

Problems on an IQ test are ranked according to the age at which the average child can solve them. The original Binet test provided a score based on the concept of mental age, the age when a child can perform tasks that have been classified into age levels through studies of large numbers of children. For example, if a four-year-old can solve problems usually solved by five-year-olds, his mental age is five; if he answers primarily questions typical of the three-year-old, his mental age is three. Binet divided a child's mental age by his chronological age and then multiplied by 100 to eliminate the decimal point. The resulting quotient became known as the intelligence quotient, or IQ.

By this scoring method, the average IQ is 100, as the average four-year-old would have a mental age as well as a chronological age of four and would thus score 100. Today, the concept is the same, although the scores are computed somewhat differently *(box, page 41)*.

A key measure of a test's validity is how well its scores correlate with scores of other tests attempting to measure the same skills and with other indices of mental ability. The Stanford-Binet and other widely used tests are considered sound ones because they correlate highly with one another.

What IQ tests cannot measure

Critics of IQ testing contend that the practice has more limitations and disadvantages than benefits. While testing can locate those youngsters likely to do well in school, it cannot predict that a student with an IQ of 120 will do better than one who has an IQ of 110. Motivation, self-esteem and self-discipline are also important in determining academic success, and the IQ test does not measure any of these qualities. Neither can it predict performance in other desirable areas — among them creativity, athletic prowess and social competence.

Above all, it must be understood by parents that the IQ test does not place a limit on a child's ability to learn. A child whose IQ score is 110 may take a longer time or have more difficulty learning a subject than a classmate who scores 130, but with high motivation and hard work, he may surpass the higher-scoring child. In addition, he may be much more talented in music, painting or other skills that indicate a type of intelligence IQ tests do not measure. Similarly, the IQ score should not place a low ceiling on a child's aspirations. IQ levels vary widely, even within professions considered learned: One study of 80 medical students, for example, revealed IQs ranging from 110 to 150.

Cultural bias in testing

Perhaps the bitterest controversy surrounding IQ testing is that of cultural bias: the fact that IQ test questions deal with words and information that, in general, reflect only the mainstream, middle-class background, known to experts as the majority culture. Critics have argued that the test does not ask questions that might reveal the types of intelligence common to children from non-middle-class segments of American society — the street smarts, specialized vocabulary and practical survival skills, for example, that may be found among poor urban black children, Puerto Ricans and American Indians but are foreign to the offspring of middle-class suburbanites.

Right or wrong, IQ scores tend to carry much heavier implications than simply predicting school achievement. Critics contend that a child who scores low because of cultural bias is destined to be dismissed as unintelligent by teachers and therefore disadvantaged within the school system. As a result of this debate, there is a growing movement among local and national education officials to downplay the importance of IQ tests. However, these tests generally predict success in school as accurately for children of the minority culture as for children of the majority — a fact that has led some to observe that the school system is as biased as the tests.

Do test scores change?

One of the most persuasive arguments against placing heavy emphasis on IQ scores is that they often fluctuate. Research has revealed that the scores of about two out of three middle-class children tend to shift upward or downward to some extent — not usually from day to day, but over a period of time.

In one long-term study for which children underwent multiple testing when they were between two and a half and 17 years of age, researchers found that one out of three individuals had scores that fluctuated as much as 30 IQ points from the highest to lowest score, and one in seven scored a spread of 40 points. Rather than many dramatic ups and downs, these changes in IQ often showed a slow, progressive increase or decrease over the years.

This suggests that parents should never think of a child as being locked into a given level of performance for life, nor should they make casual predictions about his future prospects for success based on intelligence test scores made during his early years.

Factors affecting test performance

If your youngster achieves a lower than expected score on an IQ test, either in the preschool period or during the school years, you may want to request a retest in a later year, perhaps using a different tester or a different test. This might be important if the child is being excluded from a special program — for example, a program for gifted students — on the basis of a few percentage points of IQ. There are many reasons why a child's performance might vary from one time to another on the identical IQ test. She may have been sick or she may have been having simply a bad day when the tests were given. Or perhaps she was too fatigued or restless to complete the test, did not understand the instructions properly or was uncomfortable with the testing situation.

An examiner may also be the source of the discrepancy in scores. In one-on-one testing situations, results can be affected by nuances in the way a test is administered or how items are scored. Analyzing a preschooler's test responses is a complicated process in which many factors must be considered: Her ability to process information, memory, her understanding of social situations, articulation, her level of maturity and her degree of experience may all be involved. For example, in one type of test, children are asked to put together a series of comic-strip-like pictures so that they tell a story. First, a child must understand what it means to tell a story, then she must understand chronological sequence. She must be able to translate an abstract mental concept into pictures, and finally, she may be asked to articulate what has happened in the pictures. Interpreting the test results is a highly subjective matter, and there is likely to be variation among individual testers. For school-age children, test taking is more uniform and scoring more objective, but even here testers can vary in the degree of their strictness or leniency in administering tests and in the clarity of their instructions.

New directions in testing

As a result of the acknowledged limitations of IQ tests, many educators and psychologists are beginning to explore other indicators of intelligence. Among such tests are a group of instruments known as dynamic assessment tests, which are designed to measure what a child is capable of learning during the course of the test procedure. In the standard IQ test, a child is asked to copy a circle; the score for that problem depends on whether she can or cannot do it on the first try. In a dynamic assessment test, if the child cannot copy the circle on the first try, she is shown how to do so, then asked to try it again. When she has drawn the circle, she is asked to complete a similar task. This form of testing measures the child's learning speed and her ability to transfer skills from one problem to another.

Attempts to develop tests that measure creativity have been somewhat less successful. In one such test, children are asked questions such as, "How many uses can you think of for a paper clip?" Scores are based on the number of answers the child can come up with and the novelty of the responses. Critics have pointed out, however, that such tests measure only the child's ability to give unusual answers — and that being different is not necessarily the same as being creative.

Testing infant intelligence

One of the most fascinating challenges for psychologists has been the attempt to devise ways of testing babies and toddlers: Obviously, without language as a communication tool, the only way of studying their mental behavior is to observe what they do naturally. One typical and frequently used measure of development for the very young is the Bayley Scales of Infant Development, named for Nancy Bayley, the child psychologist at the University of California at Berkeley who directed the test's development. The Bayley Scales are divided into three sections: the Motor Scale, the Mental Scale and the Infant Behavior Profile.

The Motor Scale is designed to measure control of the body and coordination. The Mental Scale assesses perception, memory, learning and problem solving. Reading emotional expressions in a baby's face is a major source of information about the child's intelligence. For example, in an exercise where the child is challenged to find hidden objects, the examiner will infer intelligence if the baby shows surprise when the object is discovered. If the infant shows persistence and curiosity in the search, this is also a sign of intelligence, indicating that the child has learned that the object did not disappear, but was simply hidden.

The Infant Behavior Profile is based on attention, motivation and sociability. At six months, intelligence is inferred from what a baby pays attention to. At 12 months, the tests evaluate how much a baby imitates the examiner, another behavior assumed to indicate intelligence. At 18 months, the major test criterion is language: how many words the child knows and whether she can put together two or three words, such as "me go" or "put on hat."

The Bayley Scales and other similar tests, usually administered by a professional examiner, are most often employed to identify children who lag far behind their age mates and who may require special attention. None of these tests reliably predict later intelligence when they are given before the child has reached two or three years of age.

Researchers have developed some measures of infant intelligence, however, that seem to correlate with later IQ scores. One approach measures a type of early learning called habituation. Scientists have found that if an infant is shown a repeated visual pattern or given a repeated sound, she will pay increasingly less attention to it; she will become bored by the sound or pattern and seek something new. The rate at which she loses interest is the rate of habituation. Follow-up studies show that babies who habituate quickly at four months usually outscore other children on IQ tests when they reach four years.

In general, those babies considered unusually intelligent by experts are not necessarily early walkers or talkers, but children who demonstrate an exceptional amount of curiosity, perceptiveness and drive. Children who are oriented toward learning and who continually scan their environment for information are regarded as more intelligent than those who are not learning oriented. Perhaps most significant, a baby's confident attitude — as indicated by positive emotional responses, eagerness to explore her environment and lack of fearfulness — is considered an important indicator of later intellectual achievement. ⁛

Common Concerns

About Children's Intelligence

My son is very creative. I was told that he must be a right-brain person. What does this mean?

The left hemisphere and the right hemisphere of the brain control different intellectual functions. The left hemisphere is concerned with spoken and written language, verbal reasoning, number skills and scientific skills. This logical, analytical side is dominant in most people, and most intelligence tests focus primarily on the workings of the left half of the brain. The right hemisphere is involved with art and music awareness, emotions, imagination and with those spatial functions that enable us to understand maps or recognize faces. Your son seems to exhibit talents that are controlled by the right side of the brain.

My oldest child has a higher IQ score than his younger brother and sister. Does birth order affect IQ?

It can, indirectly. Firstborn children often perform slightly better on verbal tests than their siblings. One probable reason is that most parents have more time to spend alone with their first child, and thus the eldest is often introduced to more intellectually stimulating activities at an early age.

My daughter was an early walker; does this mean she will have a natural gift for athletics?

No. Each child's rate of development in the early years is different and usually is not a predictor of future accomplishments. Slow developers have as good a chance of becoming successful athletes as those who develop more quickly.

Is it true that boys are naturally better at math than girls are?

Until adolescence, boys and girls do equally well at counting and at arithmetic on tests. Starting at about the age of 12, however, boys begin to outscore girls on mathematical tasks. Some experts believe that the cause is more environmental than hereditary, arguing that society's traditional view of math as masculine discourages girls from pursuing it.

Others believe there may be a biological contribution to the difference, as well.

Is there any difference between the IQ scores of boys and girls?

While comparisons of boys' and girls' scores on IQ tests show no significant difference in overall mental ability, the two sexes display different patterns of strengths and weaknesses in specific abilities. On the average, girls score slightly better on vocabulary, spelling, reading comprehension and creative writing.

Boys tend to be slightly better at solving mazes, recognizing geometric forms and depth perception.

What causes the gap in IQ scores between blacks and whites?

The reasons why whites score an average of 10 to 15 points higher than blacks is a subject of heated controversy. Some psychologists contend that the difference is genetic; others argue that social and cultural conditions prevent blacks from scoring as high on IQ tests, which are generally geared to white, middle-class experiences. Although the average scores differ, individual scores of both races cover the same numerical range of about 40 to 200 points.

As a parent, is there anything I can do to help raise my child's IQ?

In general, creating an environment that is conducive to learning helps a child grow intellectually. This includes introducing him from an early age to a variety of interesting experiences that will stimulate his curiosity. Encouraging a child to use language and to read may also help him do well.

My little girl is adopted. Will her IQ be closer to mine and my husband's or to the IQ of her natural parents?

Your youngster's IQ will reflect both hereditary and environmental factors. Studies have shown that adopted children who live in advantaged homes generally score higher on IQ tests than would be expected on the basis of heredity alone. Their scores tend to be higher than the scores of their biological mother and father.

The Gifted Child

The term "gifted child" summons up a host of contrasting images: the quick-witted charmer, the eccentric loner, the artistic or musical prodigy, or perhaps the miniature genius thrust prematurely into the society of older children. Any of these descriptions may fit, for like all children, the gifted vary widely in their interests, talents and personalities. What they all have in common is the fact that nature has endowed them with a remarkably high potential for achievement. From birth on, it is up to parents, teachers and the child's own temperament and motivation to translate that potential into accomplishment.

Who are the gifted? Obviously, it is not an easy thing to apply objective standards to the creative expressions of young minds. It is particularly difficult to detect giftedness during infancy and toddlerhood, when children's mental and physical development is still in a state of flux and cannot be taken as a reliable gauge of later ability levels. As a child grows into the preschool years, however, parents, relatives and caregivers may be delighted to observe her displaying some or many behavioral characteristics typical of gifted children *(page 49)*. But these behaviors are also displayed by children of average intelligence to varying degrees, and there are no firm guidelines for using the traits as a diagnostic tool. In fact, most experts feel that it is neither useful nor desirable for parents to attach too much importance to giftedness, or lack of it, during the preschool years.

Primarily using studies of school-age children, most authorities estimate that between 2 and 5 percent of all youngsters can be truly classified as gifted. Researchers working with gifted children have identified several different areas in which a child may shine. First, there are the children who perform extremely well on general intelligence tests. Children with IQs of 130 to 140 are usually considered to be gifted, and children with IQs over 140 are described as highly gifted.

There are other children considered gifted who do not perform as well overall on intelligence tests but have an outstanding aptitude in a specific academic field such as math or reading. Still other children are included among the gifted for their leadership ability. Starting at an early age, they seem to understand the feelings and responses of others, are adept at handling social situations and can easily take charge.

Exceptional ability in the visual or performing arts is another category of giftedness, as is a talent for creative or productive thinking — the latter, of course, being the hardest type of talent to define and measure.

Early and late bloomers Just as children possess different types of exceptional ability, they reveal that ability in widely varying patterns. Some children show signs of

Gifted children can usually learn a skill with little or no formal training — and learn it earlier than other children. Many master basic reading skills on their own, for example, using a method such as that pictured above: figuring out words on the back of a cereal box. Although his parents may have read books to him, this gifted boy is teaching himself to read.

giftedness from an early age. As infants, they gaze intently at people and objects and appear unusually alert and aware of their surroundings. They frequently reach developmental stages ahead of schedule. While the average child uses a few simple words or phrases by the age of two, the gifted child often talks in complex sentences. By four, she may have taught herself to read by observing printed words on everything from road signs to toy packages.

Other gifted children, however, do not fit this model. Though their potential may equal or exceed that of the precocious toddler or pre-schooler, their special talents do not show up until elementary school or even later. Boys, especially, tend to be late bloomers. Yet looking back, parents may recall events or traits that were clues, such as an unusually long attention span, or a tendency to ask complicated questions and demand complex, detailed answers.

Although it may seem a contradiction, some gifted children are also learning disabled *(pages 78-85)*. It has been noted that Albert Einstein, whose name has become synonymous with genius, was quite late in learning to speak and had a very poor school record in the early grades. While there are probably very few potential Einsteins going unrecognized in the classroom, it is nevertheless believed that a significant number of gifted children are overlooked or misunderstood because a specific learning problem or emotional disturbance masks their talents. Greater awareness on the part of teachers, family physicians and parents can increase the prospects that these handicapped gifted youngsters will be discovered.

Testing for exceptional abilities

Except in rare cases, testing a younger preschooler for giftedness serves no significant purpose. Results of such tests are considered more reliable once a child has reached the age of four. Some experts suggest that early testing may have detrimental effects if the parents react inappropriately to test results. For example, a parent who is aware that his toddler or preschooler is developmentally advanced, and who therefore becomes convinced that the child is gifted, may mistakenly feel the need to focus on academic pursuits for which the child is not ready.

The occasional child who may benefit from preschool testing is the emotionally disturbed or learning-disabled child whose particular problems are covering up his overall abilities. If early testing reveals that he is exceptionally advanced in other developmental areas, then parents and professionals can work together to help him cope with his problems and develop his potential to the fullest.

Whether they are early or late bloomers, most gifted youngsters are first officially designated as such by tests administered during their school years — often tests given to determine eligibility for acceptance into special gifted-pupil programs, which many public school systems now sponsor. Most such programs focus on children with high intellectual ability and academic aptitude, partly because they are the easiest to identify. To determine which youngsters are gifted, most schools rely primarily on a combination of a child's achievement and IQ scores, with

The Special Ways of a Gifted Child

Described below are some of the behavorial characteristics gifted children display during the preschool years. Keep in mind that any child may show one or more of these traits, on a frequent or occasional basis. What distinguishes the gifted child is that he shows many of them consistently and to a remarkable degree.

- A gifted child may have an extremely high energy level, especially when he is working on projects that have particular interest for him. In some cases, gifted children seem to require less sleep than other children their age.

- The gifted are often insatiably curious and have a wide range of interests and hobbies. They ask many intelligent questions about the way things work, and their questions show an ability to anticipate potential outcomes. For example, a child might ask a series of questions about making honey: "How can a bee tell which flowers have the nectar to make honey? Do the bees ever get stuck in the honey while they are making it?"

- A gifted child frequently has an unusually long attention span and an advanced ability to concentrate. She might become absorbed in a project and work through recess or dinner, barely noticing the passage of time.

- Gifted children often have remarkable memories and can retain most of what they observe or learn. If the smallest object is removed from a room, for example, a gifted child of two or three may inquire where it is.

- Gifted children often like to collect things such as rocks or bottle caps. Part of their enjoyment of this may lie in the abstract thinking involved: sorting objects, noting similarities and differences, and making judgments based on generalities.

- They may be precocious talkers, use grown-up words at an early age and converse easily with adults. Instead of saying "I saw a kitty," a gifted two-year-old might say "I saw a black-and-white kitty across the street and he was chasing a squirrel."

- Gifted children who are talented in verbal areas often enjoy playing with words and thinking up rhymes, opposites or analogies. They tend to recount events they have experienced, or they may retell in great detail stories that were told to them.

- Often, they can create short stories, poems and letters at an early age. For example, a child might dictate a letter to his mother at the age of three.

- In many cases, gifted children teach themselves to read. For example, a three-year-old might surprise her parents on a car trip by reading the road signs to them. A child of four might be discovered reading books at the second-grade level.

- Gifted children frequently have rich fantasies and develop relationships with imaginary playmates.

- They may have a mature sense of humor, understand when they are being teased and know how to tease back. Gifted children may see the humor in jokes and puns that other children do not understand.

- Gifted children may develop elaborate theories about the way things work — notions that are based on observation and deduction as well as on careful questioning.

- They often prefer to play with older children and they get along well with adults. At the same time, gifted children can enjoy playing or working on a project alone.

- A gifted child may be fascinated with clocks and calendars and understand how they work ahead of other children her age. She may learn to count early and show an interest in other mathematical concepts as well.

- A gifted youngster may be quick to understand cause-and-effect relationships, and she may speculate about what might happen: "If we put out some sugar and water, could the bees use it to make honey?"

- Gifted children arrive at abstract thinking at an earlier age, and they are often interested in philosophical issues such as injustice.

- Gifted children may remember the various pitches of a sequence of musical notes, and they may sing songs in perfect tune at an early age.

- They may be unusually sensitive to the feelings of others and have an intuitive understanding of a parent's or a playmate's sadness or anger. Sometimes this is manifested as sympathy and concern for the plight of people they do not know but have heard about.

- Often gifted children can put seemingly unrelated objects or ideas together to make new combinations. In this way, they develop imaginative and original solutions to problems.

consideration given as well to the child's emotional and social abilities.

In some programs, children who are not among the upper 5 percent in intelligence tests but show themselves to be academically talented are also included. Where this criterion is accepted, it expands the concept of a gifted group considerably, often up to 15 to 20 percent of the school population.

Adjustment problems

The stereotyped image of the child prodigy as a gawky misfit hardly fits the majority of gifted children. Exceptionally talented youngsters are generally well adjusted and well liked by their peers. They often become self-reliant at an earlier stage than other children. Because they can succeed more easily at tasks, they tend to suffer fewer frustrations than their peers, to see themselves early in life as a source of pride to their parents and to enjoy high self-esteem.

However, gifted children are different from other children in certain respects. They often seem older than their years, and they tend to be more questioning and philosophical in their outlook on life. These differences may give rise to problems for the gifted child in the classroom, on the playground and at home.

A gifted preschooler may be advanced intellectually, but he often acts his age emotionally. As a result, parents and teachers may sometimes put excessive demands on his behavior, expecting him to act more mature than he really is. Also, during the preschool years when his creative abilities may far surpass his manual dexterity, he may become easily frustrated if he cannot carry through with his hands a project he has envisioned in his mind.

The gap between his intellectual and chronological age also puts him in a difficult position with other children. Some gifted children suppress their talents in order to fit in with their peers. Others withdraw and become loners, or gravitate toward older children. But a child who is smaller and less physically able than older companions may develop a passive personality or feelings of inadequacy.

Problems for the gifted child may also arise in school. Many tend to be nonconformist thinkers or to demonstrate an intensity that rubs teachers the wrong way. If bored in the classroom, they may daydream or make mischief. And an exceptionally bright child may not do well on routine schoolwork and on tests if his divergent, creative style of thinking produces several ideas and solutions instead of the one right answer the teacher is looking for.

Living with a gifted child

Many parents react to the discovery that their child is gifted with a mixture of pride and concern. They are pleased that he has been recognized as special, yet they may also worry about how his giftedness will affect other aspects of his life. Or they are intimidated by his potential and worry that they are not doing the right things to develop it.

To be sure, a gifted child will probably demand more of your time than an average child would, and you will want to stimulate him with ideas and activities that are challenging enough to hold his interest —

even if they seem far too old for him. For example, if he is intrigued by dinosaurs, you might take him to a museum that has prehistoric fossils or perhaps help him mold dinosaurs out of clay.

At the same time, you do not need to go overboard in finding ways to keep him busy developing his interests. He also needs to have ample quiet time alone, for thinking and daydreaming. These periods when he seems to be doing nothing may be the very moments that spawn creative insights.

Perhaps the most valuable thing you can do for him is to be a good and patient listener. Gifted children are generally great talkers; they often develop detailed theories about what they have observed and seek answers to long strings of complex questions. One mother of a gifted child admitted she was guilty of halfhearted listening until the day her three-year-old son grabbed her face with his small hands and insisted: "Mommy, listen to me with your eyes."

Avoiding parental pitfalls

Although your gifted child needs the freedom to explore and experiment, do not make the mistake of being overly permissive or indulgent because of his exceptional talents. A child who is led to believe that he is entitled to special treatment and rewards may develop a superior attitude that will only handicap him in later life. Many gifted and talented youngsters have fallen by the wayside simply because they expected everything to come easily and did not learn early the importance of hard work, self-discipline and commitment to achieving goals.

Some parents also develop excessively high expectations of their gifted child and feel disappointed if he does not live up to them. It is important to recognize the fine line between encouraging a child to do his best and expecting him to be perfect and to excel at everything he does. Such demands can arouse feelings of anger and guilt in the child, who begins to see his worth as dependent on how well he performs. Some gifted children become chronic underachievers as a way of rebelling against parental pressure.

As a parent you should keep in mind, above all, that a gifted child is still a child. Like any other youngster, he needs encouragement and stimulation, plenty of time for physical activity and play, and the continual reassurance that his parents love and accept him for himself alone, not for the talents he displays. ∴

For parents, challenging a gifted child with activities that keep pace with her interests and ability levels can be a challenge all its own. Here, a young girl plays a game of chess with her mother — bringing into play memory skills, a grasp of spatial relationships and abstract reasoning abilities far beyond the capacities of most children her age.

3 The Developing Mind

For a short time, new babies seem more like small animals than future thinking beings. They start out with very few learning tools — some newborn reflexes, their sensory organs, an immature nervous system and a potent but, thus far, only partially developed brain *(pages 56-57)*. In the first weeks after birth, it is really a baby's innate reflexes that exert the dominant control; however, learning is constantly taking place. Every new experience and every person or object a baby encounters helps expand her store of information and lay the groundwork for obtaining future knowledge.

The earliest years are a time of unsurpassed intellectual growth. To achieve the simple feat of writing her own name, the five-year-old at right has mastered a remarkable succession of mental skills, including shape recognition, a perception of alphabet letters as a way of communicating, the ability to store the letters of her name in memory and to retrieve them, an understanding of the relationship between written words and language and, not least, a firm and proud sense of her own identity.

This section of the book outlines in chart form these and other developmental achievements: the milestones of cognitive growth that transform a youngster's thinking as she evolves from an infant into a school-age child. To communicate successfully with your youngster throughout these early years, you must constantly remind yourself that her whole way of thinking is very different from your own. Try to stay in tune with the sometimes narrow, sometimes wildly expansive and often magical ways in which she perceives the world. And as you teach and guide her, be sensitive to the rapidly changing levels at which she is able to learn.

Building a Set of Mental Skills

Many parents tend to equate cognitive development with such learning milestones as starting to read, count or recite the alphabet. While the phrase does encompass such accomplishments, it means a great deal more besides. Simply stated, cognitive development is the growth of a child's basic mental skills — his ability to perceive and remember, to reason and imagine. It is the process by which a youngster acquires knowledge and understanding of the world around him, and also the way he learns to plan, anticipate and choose a course of action to meet the changing demands of that world. The process begins at birth and advances rapidly during the first few years, fueled by the richness of the child's surroundings and his ability to adapt to new situations.

How learning begins

To understand cognitive development, it helps to contrast the many ways in which adults acquire knowledge and the relatively few ways, at first, in which a baby can learn. Adults learn through experimentation, observation and imitation, as well as by asking questions, reasoning and using intuition. A baby starts out solely with instincts, then proceeds to master all of the other learning skills step by step.

Think of your baby's mind as a system — undeveloped at first — that absorbs, processes and transforms information and stimuli collected by the senses. Because he cannot use language to communicate and has few past experiences to serve as reference points, his thought processes are very simple to begin with. If it were possible to peer inside his mind, you would probably see a series of isolated visual images and unrelated sounds.

Cognitive growth begins with the five senses and the inborn physical reflexes — among them sucking, crying and grasping. As simple and primitive as these reflexes are, they are enough to start your infant learning. He instinctively repeats and practices the few skills he has: He roots for the breast, waves his arms and legs, and cries to express his needs. In doing so, he is brought face to face with the world around him. When he roots on his father's shoulder he does not find food, only affection and a scratchy chin. When he thrashes his arms in his cradle, he discovers the toys that you left to amuse him. His cries sometimes bring you to his bedside and sometimes bring unfamiliar faces — an aunt, perhaps, or a baby-sitter. He develops new ways of responding and new ways of thinking in order to cope with each new experience — the fundamental pattern of cognitive growth.

Piaget's theories of development

Much of what is known today about the ways children come to understand the world stems from the work of Jean Piaget, a Swiss psychologist whose writings between 1923 and 1976 revolutionized the study of cognition. Piaget grew up in a society where young children were generally regarded as miniature adults, with mental processes that were a scaled-down version of grown-up thinking. But he began to question this view during his first job in Paris as a postgraduate student: Working as an intelligence tester for Alfred Binet, the grandfather of the modern-day IQ test *(page 40),* Piaget became intrigued by the incorrect re-

"What happens when you knock over the first domino in the line?" So begins, for this curious preschooler, a lesson in cause and effect — just one of the many steps in his development of logic and reasoning. During the early years of life, hands-on experimentation is one of the chief ways in which children learn.

sponses young children gave to certain test questions. He saw similarities in the wrong answers given by children of the same age and wondered about the mental patterns that produced those responses.

In addition to his observations at Binet's laboratory school, Piaget began to study his own three children — Laurent, Jacqueline and Lucienne — in play situations. After years of charting their day-to-day activities in minute detail, he proposed theories outlining the ways all children learn to adapt and organize their behavior.

Piaget concluded, in essence, that children develop primarily by interacting with the world around them. He viewed children as intellectually curious by nature, with an insatiable appetite for learning and a strong need to understand what they see. He believed that they learn by doing and that — in their characteristically egocentric fashion — they can perceive the world only in the way they themselves have experienced it.

Although some subsequent scholars have developed modified versions of Piaget's views and have taken different approaches to the subject of human learning, Piaget's theories remain at the core of modern cognitive studies.

Assimilation and accommodation

Piaget saw learning as the product of a child's constantly adapting to the demands of the world. His model of cognitive growth is built around two fundamental concepts, assimilation and accommodation. These he viewed as opposite but complementary parts of the process of adaptation. When a child encounters something new, whether it is a bright light, a strange face or a new kind of animal, he assimilates it; that is, he adds it to the repertoire of things he already knows. At the same time, he is forced to change, or accommodate, his thinking and behavior to allow for the differences he finds in the new object. He must make the new information fit with his preconceived notions of the world and, if necessary, create a new mental category in which to store it.

For example, a child who sees an elephant for the first time may think of it as a horse, because up to that point horses were the largest animals he had ever seen. When he observes that the elephant is not really like a horse but is a much larger animal with wide, floppy ears and an extraordinarily long nose, he accommodates this new information into his mental storehouse. He realizes that there are animals even bigger than horses. His notion of animals has changed: It still is not perfect, but it has been refined. He has pushed his mind a little further, taken another step in his mental development. According to Piaget, knowledge is acquired in small steps like these, each of them giving the child new reference points for dealing with the next new experience.

Forming mental patterns

This fluid process of assimilating and accommodating new information leads the child to form mental patterns — what Piaget called schemata.

How a Child's Brain Matures

In the early years of life, a youngster's ability to learn is closely tied to patterns of physical development in the brain. Although most of the essential apparatus that makes learning possible is in place by the time a baby is born, critical connections remain to be formed. The order in which those developments occur helps to explain the predictable sequence in which children master such basic skills as crawling, walking and speaking.

The disproportionately large head of the newborn — which is one of the baby's most distinctive features — is explained by the remarkably hefty brain that resides within: At birth, the organ is already one quarter its eventual adult weight, outsized for a body that is only about one twentieth its potential weight. The brain continues to grow rapidly; it will reach about 90 percent of full growth by the time the youngster is six years old.

The brain is made up of two types of cells: nerve cells, which transmit and receive messages, and support cells, which nourish and protect the nerve cells. By the time of birth, the brain has nearly all of the 20 billion or so nerve cells that it will ever have. These early nerve cells are simple, however, and relatively isolated from each other. It is during the first year of a child's life that each nerve cell develops the 1,000 to 100,000 connections with other nerve cells in the brain that give humans their unique associative powers (*illustration, right*).

Most of the growth in the brain after birth involves support cells rather than new nerve cells. In addition to their other functions, support cells direct the production of a fatty, white substance called myelin that sheathes the nerve cells and makes possible efficient transmission of the electrochemical signals by which the cells communicate. The effect of the myelin is much like that of in-

sulation on electrical wires: It keeps the current from leaving its path. Thus, a newborn baby's brain has not only to establish the connections between its billions of nerve cells, but it must grow new tissue in order to become efficient at conveying messages through the new connections.

The blossoming of the baby's mind and body proceeds in lock step with these developments. For example, one of the parts of the brain where the myelin is well developed at birth is the part that will control movement of the upper body. As a result, a baby learns to lift his head and to play with his hands before he can control his legs or lower body. Speech, on the other hand, cannot commence until the part of the brain involved in hearing has developed, as well as parts that give the child motor control over the lips, tongue and jaw, and this happens much later.

Nerve cells and support cells form the many distinct sections of the brain responsi-

ble for different mental and physical functions (*illustration, opposite*). These sections mature in a predictable pattern: In general, development progresses from sections that control the basic life functions — such as breathing, swallowing and blood circulation — to those sections that control more complicated motor activities and sensory functions.

The last parts of the brain to mature are those that control the higher brain functions, such as memory and creativity. In physical terms, development proceeds from the top of the spinal column, upward and outward to the top of the brain.

Because most of an infant's mental and physical abilities up to the age of 18 months are the result of this biological maturation process, learning specialists claim that all normal infants, as long as they are given proper nutrition and a normal, active environment, will develop predictable skills in a predictable sequence. Although this learning process may proceed at different rates in different children, there is little that parents can do to accelerate the biological growth of their children.

The relevant message for parents in this brief anatomy lesson is that nature cannot be rushed when it comes to early childhood learning: It is futile to try to teach a youngster to walk, to play the piano or to memorize nursery rhymes before his brain has developed the necessary pathways and has made the appropriate connections to support such learning breakthroughs.

Instead, it is best to simply stay in tune with your youngster's ever-changing capabilities: Seek ways to challenge him with activities that seem to satisfy his hunger to exercise newly won physical skills and mental abilities, but at the same time, be careful not to expect more performance from your child than nature has enabled him to deliver.

The Network of Nerve-Cell Connections

As suggested by the schematic drawing below, left, the nerve cells in the brain of a newborn baby have relatively few connections with other nerve cells. By the time the child is six years old, however, each cell has connections numbering in the tens of thousands (below, right). The growth of this vast network makes possible the explosion of physical and mental development that marks a child's early years.

Birth

Six years

A center for sensory control

Shortly after birth, development begins within the cerebral cortex, the outermost section of the brain and the last to mature. All of the sense organs are already functioning, but the brain is not ready to make full use of their capacities. For example, a newborn's ears are fully formed, but it takes several months before the child is able to turn directly toward the source of a sound. The early growth of sensory acuity is essential to learning, because the senses are the child's only source of information.

Headquarters for higher brain functions

As time goes on, more and more bodily activities come under the control of the cerebral cortex. Primitive reflexes begin to disappear around the third month, as the developing cortex overrides the lower motor centers. The cortex is responsible for the higher conceptual functions. It is this section that makes a child uniquely human — allowing him to remember the past, imagine the future, find solutions to problems and create ideas.

The motor center

The cerebellum receives signals from muscles, joints, tendons and the inner ears. It organizes the body's motor activities, maintaining posture, coordinating major muscle movements and inhibiting unwanted movements. Reaching for a small object, for example, requires a complex series of muscle movements orchestrated by the cerebellum: While it controls the stretching hand, it must also adjust the body to maintain balance and inhibit unwanted muscle activity that would cause the hand to shake. Such complex muscle control is not possible at birth but must develop quickly in order for learning to progress.

A vital functions center

Many of the most basic life processes are controlled by a bulbous extension of the spinal cord that extends deep into the brain. Called the brainstem, this primitive section of the brain controls the baby's breathing, swallowing, blood pressure, hunger pangs and other vital functions. The brain cells in the brainstem are myelinated at birth; thus, babies are born with these complex life-sustaining systems already up and running.

SENSORY FUNCTIONS

cerebral cortex

CONCEPTUAL FUNCTIONS

brainstem

MOTOR COORDINATION

cerebellum

VITAL FUNCTIONS

These patterns can be simple mental images or patterns of actions that the child calls forth in response to day-to-day events. For instance, when the youngster first learns to crawl up the stairs to his bedroom, he establishes a mental pattern that includes all of the muscle movements needed to stay balanced while hoisting himself up the tall steps. He then uses this same mental pattern to climb other stairways, not just the one that leads to his room.

Such mental patterns also help the child organize and interpret the messages of his senses. Snatches of a bird's song, the flavor of ice cream, even a distinctive smell can bring back remembered mental images. Walking past a carnival and hearing the music of a calliope may trigger a mental picture of riding the merry-go-round. And when the youngster begins to talk, each new word establishes mental patterns and organizes many associations. The word "car" may bring together many different ideas — big black tires, loud noises on the street, a breeze through his hair, a quickly changing view, his father's eyes in the rearview mirror.

In the early years of learning, the youngster's mental patterns are constantly being refined or replaced. In many ways, it is the changes in these mental patterns that best define your youngster's cognitive growth and development.

Stages of cognitive growth

Along with his theories of assimilation, accommodation and schemata, Piaget suggested that a child's early development proceeds in distinct stages, each of which represents a fundamental shift in the youngster's conceptual abilities. Although some children reach certain stages earlier than others, every child must go through each stage before he can proceed to the next one. The order of the stages never varies, regardless of differences in culture or social class. At each stage the child learns about the world in slightly more sophisticated ways and has slightly more advanced ways of organizing his thinking. The skills the child learns in each new stage serve as steppingstones to new ways of thinking.

The stages of mental development outlined in the chart on pages 62-77 are based on periods defined by Piaget. He divided the years before a child enters school into two larger periods: the time between birth and the age of 24 months, which he called the sensory-motor period; and the time from two through seven years, which he labeled the preoperational period. For each of these phases, Piaget described advances in the areas of language, play and morality and in the child's ability to understand the concepts of time, space and numbers *(box, right)*.

The sensory-motor period

In the first phase of cognitive growth, your child does not so much think as react. He responds to his environment, attempting to control or affect it. The youngster moves beyond this reactive approach to the world when he learns that he can take some matters into his own hands. When he reaches out for your finger or an object he wants, he is beginning to act intentionally.

Patterns of Learning Traced by Piaget

Pioneer child psychologist and cognitive theorist Jean Piaget saw mental growth as proceeding on many different fronts simultaneously. He viewed six areas of learning — language, morality, play, numbers, space and time — as particularly significant, and he wrote extensively on the patterns of development in those areas.

Language

Piaget observed that children first use speech for purposes other than communicating. In the beginning, a child's vocalizations are entirely egocentric: She does not care whether anyone is listening or whether her sounds make sense to other people. The child repeats her favorite sounds simply for the enjoyment of hearing them.

Later, when the child is capable of using simple sentences, she may indulge in long monologues, jumping from idea to idea without concern for logic or sense. In the last stages of this purely egocentric speech, she may engage in what Piaget called "collective monologues" — chattering at length with other children without actually listening to what the others are saying.

As the youngster gets older, she becomes more socialized and her speech patterns change to accommodate her need to communicate. Her conversations continue to be one-sided, but she is now much more likely to respond to what another person is saying.

Morality

By studying children of various ages playing games, Piaget noted that moral awareness — specifically, a child's respect for a system of rules — increases in stages, paralleling learning in other areas. He observed that children up to the age of two years simply play with objects at will, with no concept of rules. As preschoolers, they begin to have some grasp of how rules work to organize a game but play in typically egocentric fashion, often changing the rules to suit their mood at the moment. Around the age of seven, a child enters a stage in which he unquestioningly accepts rules and guidelines laid down by adults and will follow them to the letter. Only later will he begin to consider the underlying purposes of rules and discipline himself to follow them.

Play

Almost as soon as an infant can perceive her surroundings, imitation becomes the common thread running through her play. Imitation starts as simple copying of sounds, gestures and facial expressions. For some time, the baby may not even understand the actions that she is copying. She may wave good-by when you enter a room, for example. But gradually her imitations become both complex and appropriate, relying less and less on trial and error.

The youngster's earliest forms of imitation evolve into two types of activity, which Piaget identified as "practice play" and "symbolic play," paralleling the two major phases of early childhood. Practice play predominates during the sensory-motor phase, when the child is busy learning physical skills and integrating the messages of her senses. This is purely physical activity, with no rules or structure. In addition to such activities as swinging, running or jumping, practice play can involve the senses — especially taste, smell and hearing. There is no purpose to this behavior other than the enjoyable sensations it provides.

Symbolic play commences at about the age of two, when fantasy and imagination begin to flower. Previously, the child ran for the pure pleasure of running; now, in the preoperational stage, she may run because she is a galloping horse or a jet speeding across the sky. Symbolic play serves many purposes: It helps the child learn to distinguish between what is real and unreal; it lets her practice emotions or reenact experiences that have frightened her to make them seem less intimidating; and it gives her a forum in which she has total control.

Numbers

Children commonly learn to recite numbers by rote before they understand their meaning and proper use; numerals — two or six or nine — are, at first, simply words or objects to a preschooler. His early style of perception tends to confuse his sense of numbers, along with other logical concepts, because he is able to focus only on one aspect of a situation at a time. For example, if a child of three or four is shown two rows of 10 pennies — one stretched out long, one bunched up short — he will most likely say there are more pennies in the longer row. He is focusing exclusively on the external appearance of the rows and cannot understand that quantities remain the same despite changes in outward appearances — a principle that Piaget called conservation. It is around the time they enter school that children grasp this concept, which is the basis for their understanding that a number serves as a symbol for a fixed quantity of objects — whatever their arrangement.

Space

Babies start with a very limited concept of shapes and spatial relationships; they build this understanding slowly, by handling the objects around them and, later, by moving among them as they crawl and walk. Piaget found that a child's perceptions of objects in space are profoundly affected by her egocentric world view: In the early preschool years, she can visualize an object only from her own perspective at a given moment and cannot envision the same object from someone else's angle of vision. As her egocentrism becomes less pronounced, around the age of six, she begins to adjust her perspective and understand that the same object can look different from different points of view.

Time

A child's understanding of time takes a long while to mature. As a newborn, he lives exclusively in the present; throughout his first two years, his developing memory gives him a slowly growing awareness of past events. But it is not until the age of five or so that the concept of the future takes hold. A preschooler's idea of time is generally intertwined with other concepts such as distance, place and speed. His idea of an hour may be the distance to grandmother's house; dinnertime is whenever he is eating dinner. Fast is when he puts away his blocks real fast, and slow is when he takes his time. Usually a child has reached school age before he grasps the notion of time as a continuous flow and is able to tell time by the clock.

During this phase, your child's desire to repeat or prolong the experiences that he enjoys drives him to master new skills. He mainly learns, however, through a direct, physical process of trial and error. If he likes the sound he hears when he shakes his toy bell, he may shake everything he finds in hopes of reproducing the sound. The first glimpses of intelligence are revealed when the child looks for new ways to accomplish what he wants, such as tapping on the bell with a stick or another toy.

The end of the sensory-motor phase is marked by the beginnings of mental trial and error in place of strictly hands-on experimentation. This capacity for rudimentary abstract thought is linked to advances in the child's understanding of his own identity in relation to the external world. In particular, the child must realize that objects and other people have an existence of their own. This sense of what is referred to as "object permanence" — that objects have a permanent existence even though they cannot be seen — is the beginning of the process of learning through mental imagery. The youngster now has the ability to think about things without actually having them in front of his eyes.

The preoperational period

Trial and error is still the primary mode of learning in the second phase of cognitive growth. But it is trial and error on a completely different level of operation. After the age of two years, your child is rapidly learning to talk and is approaching the world armed with his own ever-changing set of mental images and symbols. He has a whole new arena for his experimentation — the arena of make-believe play. Imagination now dominates his existence as he constantly tries out and refines his ideas. If the child does not know the explanation for something, he makes one up — and will stick to it until he finds something better.

He also bombards you with a nonstop barrage of questions. He is growing more and more aware of you and of the other people around him; yet, at the same time, the child seems lost in his own little world. It is during the preoperational phase that your youngster's way of thinking and looking at the world surrounding him is most different from your own.

By relating everything around him to himself, your preschooler gradually refines his sense of who he is. This self-awareness further encourages him to try as many new things as he can on his own. He is becoming an independent person, and he wants recognition for his achievements.

Suddenly the child wants to do everything at once — to walk up the stairs, to talk, to dress himself, to point to all the objects he knows and to repeat their names over and over. And so he should, for everything your youngster encounters in these expansive years is a new challenge and a potential building block of knowledge. He can store these experiences away and use them as reference points to help him in his next encounter. That is how he learns. •:•

Milestones of Cognitive Growth

Like the whorls of his fingerprints, the patterns of your youngster's mental development will prove to be unique. Just about the only sure thing you can expect is the unexpected. He may leap ahead in mastery of puzzle solving, yet be slow to attach names to the objects he handles. He may make great advances in some months, little in others. Whatever his style, however, your child — and, surprisingly perhaps, just about all other children — will progress from birth to the age of six through the same eight stages of mental development. These stages are described and illustrated in the chart that follows.

Each stage of the chart is demarcated by the range of chronological ages it represents. At first your baby may not seem to do much more than coo contentedly or give you a smile, which of itself can be a great reward. These early learning stages take only a few weeks or months. Later stages span longer periods of time and encompass the development of more complex, purposeful behavior on your child's part — such as simple problem solving at 18 to 24 months or taking heed of the implications of his own actions at four to six years.

Some of the major mental accomplishments that you can look for at each stage are set off in a box in each section of the chart, for easy reference. A second box in each section gives suggestions for learning activities that you and your youngster can take part in together.

To make the most of these pursuits, choose playtimes when your youngster is well rested and alert. In addition, be sure to reward the child's achievements with praise and affection. And — perhaps most important — you should stop the activity the moment he begins to weary. Because his attention span is quite short, your infant may tend to get fussy if a game lasts more than a minute or two. As the child grows to a toddler, these guidelines will still apply, although his energy and talent levels undoubtedly will be much higher.

Remember that children develop in highly individual patterns and that your youngster is not likely to conform to the chart at every stage of his development. But these reference norms reflect the averages and will stand you in good stead as benchmarks for judging your child's progress in the years before he goes to school.

Building on Inborn Reflexes

BIRTH TO 1 MONTH

	1 YEAR	2 YEARS	3 YEARS	4 YEARS	5 YEARS	6 YEARS

Energetically waving his arms and legs, your newborn seems to be intent on something important. But during the first month of life, a baby's movements are random — and, in many cases, reflexive. His reflexes have been well exercised in the womb. He is born able to kick, stretch, grasp, yawn, sneeze, blink, cough, grimace, suck and swallow, as well as sound off on a scale of noises from cooing to cranky.

Some reflexes, such as sneezing, will remain unchanged with age and have no relationship to learning. Others, such as moving the eyes or the hands and arms, will be trained and refined through repetition. These reflexes are the first building blocks of cognitive growth.

Although he is only awake and alert for about 20 minutes at a time, and able to see best within a focal range of eight to 18 inches, your baby has — from the moment of birth — the ability to learn. You can help him by letting him practice reflexive movements such as grasping *(below)* that soon will enable him to begin learning about the world.

Accomplishments

- Uses distinctive cries to signal his needs in different situations, such as hunger, anger or discomfort.

- Will sometimes show pleasure or contentment by cooing or making other throaty noises.

- Startles when he hears a loud noise, but may not react when he hears the noise again. Acclimates to household noises.

- Begins to quiet down and listen attentively when he hears soft, high-pitched sounds and voices.

- From birth, has the ability to discriminate among different tastes and smells — often using these senses to identify his mother and her breast milk.

- May turn his head in the direction of a source of light.

- Will peer intently at faces, particularly the eyes.

- Through a process of repetition, gradually becomes increasingly adept at reflexive acts, such as locating the nipple to begin nursing.

Helping Him Learn to Hold On

Passing toys to your baby will enhance his ability to grasp objects. Hold a small toy such as a rattle a few inches from his face to let him see it, then touch the toy against his palm; reflexes will make his fingers close around it. Let him try to hold it alone. When the toy falls, talk soothingly and repeat the game two or three times. Gradually his fingers will be strong enough to hold the toy fast. Other suitable diversions for newborns include boldly patterned pictures and music boxes.

Following the movement of a colorful rattle, the infant uses both his eyes and his ears. From birth, a baby learns about the world through his senses.

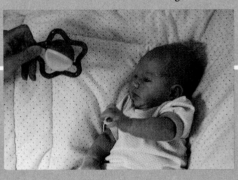

Sucking is an infant's most essential reflex. He uses this inborn skill primarily to take in nourishment, but also to calm himself by sucking on his fist or fingers.

Crying is an infant's first way of communicating. Within the first weeks, there are discernible variations — lusty cries of hunger, piercing wails of pain and fitful squalls of fatigue.

Using the Senses Together

As the baby settles in at home, his wakeful periods last longer and he is able to see objects farther away. Opportunities to learn expand with his growing ability to gain information by using two or more senses together — combining vision and hearing, for example, to locate the source of a sound. Between one and four months of age, however, most of his perceptions revolve around himself and his own body. After about two months, he discovers his hands and frequently stares at them with fascination. Gradually, he explores the rest of his body with his hands.

What have been solely random body movements now show the first signs of becoming intentional. He reaches out to grasp at the breast or bottle, at your face and hands, at toys dangled over his head. He follows you with his eyes and may imitate your expressions. He listens acutely, turning his head toward your voice, and he responds with his own growing vocabulary of squeals, coos and laughs.

By four months, anticipatory behavior is established: When he sees a bottle, he may smile and make suckling noises.

Accomplishments

- Watches the eyes and mouth of a speaker and may listen attentively to a voice for about 30 seconds.

- By two to three months of age, may turn eyes and head toward a familiar voice.

- Between two and three months, begins to look and smile directly at people; by four months, laughs aloud.

- By three to four months of age, cries much less and more purposefully; develops a special cry or other sounds to attract attention.

- Begins to babble, vocalizing vowel sounds such as "ah" and "ee," especially in response to his mother's voice.

- Recognizes toys and shows the excitement of his anticipation by kicking legs, waving arms, smiling.

- Brings everything that he is able to grasp into his mouth for exploration.

- Will repeat a newly learned activity that brings pleasure, such as shaking a rattle.

- Increasingly able to track moving objects with his eyes; by two months begins to focus on objects at different distances and by four months can see as well as an adult.

- Begins to notice differences among shapes and forms; may stare at an object for one minute or longer.

Changing Shapes and Sounds

In the course of day-to-day care of your infant, look for ways to exercise the child's fledgling perceptive powers. Hang a toy or stuffed animal within reach where he sits or over his changing table. Choose colorful playthings for your baby, especially those that make sounds when you squeeze or strike them. And use a different toy every few days — your baby will begin to notice the changes as he grows. If you use a mobile, you should change the hanging parts from time to time. Good toys for children this age include teething rings, unbreakable mirrors and bells that attach firmly to the child's wrists.

When a baby brings an object to his mouth, he learns its shape, texture and taste. By comparing these qualities to those of his fingers, he distinguishes between himself and his environment.

The infant looks and listens while his mother smiles and talks. He may babble, smile or laugh in response.

Discovering that his kicking creates an interesting result — splashing water — he gleefully repeats the action, time after time.

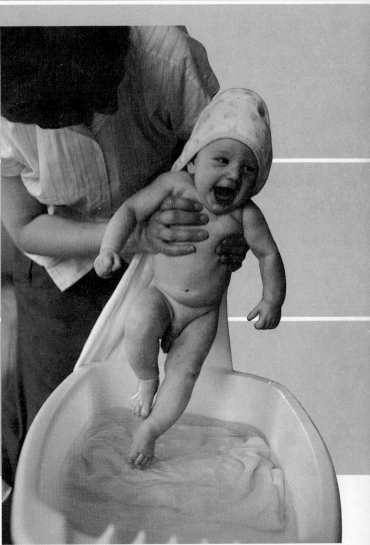

Beginning to Explore Objects

4 TO 8 MONTHS

| 1 YEAR | 2 YEARS | 3 YEARS | 4 YEARS | 5 YEARS | 6 YEARS |

Until the age of four months or so, your baby's focus has been on herself. She has had to repeat activities to become efficient — even needing to look long and hard at your face to see you well. Between four and eight months, her perceptual abilities are maturing: The more she sees, the more curious she becomes and the more responsive she is to what she finds.

Your baby may be awake and attentive for two hours or more at a stretch, giving her more time to investigate her surroundings. As her eye-hand coordination improves, she can grasp objects well, pull them toward herself and transfer them from hand to hand. Ever on the lookout for new adventures, she inspects, shakes, bangs and rattles whatever comes her way. She is discovering the effects she can have on the things around her.

As yet, her curiosity outstrips her ability to explore. But she is beginning to roll over and trying hard to crawl. She delights in new surroundings — the garden, the sandbox, the wading pool. By six or seven months, she can sit erect to survey what she finds an ever more exciting world.

Accomplishments

- Babbles spontaneously to herself. At about five months, vocalizes pleasure and displeasure.

- Recognizes familiar faces and voices by about six months; may become shy of strangers.

- Differentiates between objects and may recognize familiar ones, such as her bottle or pacifier.

- Begins to understand that objects have stable characteristics; for example, a ball's shape does not change although it may look smaller when far away.

- Turns head and shoulders in order to locate the source of a sound or voice.

- At seven months, is likely to respond to her own name; by about eight months of age, looks around for family members or pets when they are named.

- Increasingly tries to mimic parents' hand motions, facial expressions and sounds.

- Vocalizes double consonants such as "dada," "mama" and "baba" and may repeat them again and again; may consistently use a certain sound when referring to a specific person, pet or activity.

- Plays two to three minutes with a single toy.

- By about eight months, begins to understand that objects have a permanent existence. Will search briefly for objects that are dropped or hidden from view.

- Begins to understand the effects of her actions. When she drops, throws, kicks or pushes an object, she can anticipate the results.

- Reaches for something she wants and works to get it even if the object is out of reach.

Hunting for Hidden Toys

Searching for partially hidden toys is a simple game for your baby to learn and one that will give her a real sense of achieving a goal. More important, the game helps illustrate the principle that objects not visible still exist — a notion that is crucial to later stages of learning. When you are conducting the treasure-hunt game, let your baby watch you hide the toy and be sure to leave enough of it visible so that it is easy to find. When she finds the treasure, praise her and give her a hug. Peekaboo games reinforce the lessons of the treasure hunt. Other classics for children this age are action rhymes such as "Pat-a-Cake" and "This Little Piggy Went to Market." By the fifth month, your baby may enjoy being held up to look at your reflections in a mirror. Good play equipment for this stage includes an activity box for manipulating, rolling toys, cloth dolls and stuffed animals, cardboard books that have simple bright pictures, and cause-and-effect toys such as pop-up boxes or roly-poly dolls.

Already holding one toy, the child reaches for a second. Improvements in her eye-hand coordination enable her to reach quickly and smoothly for objects.

By eight months, the youngster turns both head and shoulders to locate the source of a voice.

As the baby's interest in the things around her increases, so does her attention span: She may stare at a toy for two to three minutes at a time. She shakes the toy to hear its noise, bangs it on her feeding tray, fingers it and puts it in her mouth.

Showing Purposeful Behavior

8 TO 12 MONTHS

| 1 YEAR | 2 YEARS | 3 YEARS | 4 YEARS | 5 YEARS | 6 YEARS |

Liberated by breakthroughs in his physical abilities that enable him to crawl and later to walk, your baby sets out to explore every corner of the house. Curiosity and excitement are obvious as he tries to ransack the kitchen cupboards and empty your bottom shelves. With his new mobility comes a greater awareness of the three-dimensional space around him; he can now move about a room with more assurance. When the child is about eight to 12 months, the most prominent mental development is the flowering of intentional behavior. When he crawls or cruises, he often has a distinct goal in sight: He is headed for a toy on the floor, perhaps, or to his father for a hug.

The newly obvious purpose behind his behavior is clear when he pulls at your hand for the food he wants but pushes away what he dislikes. As memory develops further, he may try familiar actions to reach his new goals: To make a noise, he shakes a rattle. But when the familiar actions do not work, he may try something new. He shakes the ball but it does not make a noise, so he rolls the ball instead.

Accomplishments

- Shows more and more intentional, goal-oriented behavior; may retrieve an object in order to resume an activity.

- Can imitate actions he has observed others perform — actions he cannot see himself do, such as opening and closing his eyes. May indicate his wishes by imitating movements involved — leaning forward when he wants you to push the stroller.

- Learns that the same action will produce different results depending on the qualities of the objects involved — a ball will bounce on the floor but splash in the water.

- By nine months, understands some words and may address parents as "mama" and "dada." By 10 months, begins to understand "no" and simple commands such as "Give it to me."

- Around 11 months, may use a few simple words such as "bye-bye"; understands the meanings of many others.

- Associates words with gestures, such as waving to say good-by; indicates desires by pointing and gesturing.

- Learns about spatial relationships through play; grasps concepts such as "full" and "empty," "up" and "down."

- May be able to stack blocks. Takes stacking rings off the spindle; by 11 months may replace the rings, although in random order. Places cylinders in matching holes in a sorting box.

- Shows first signs of ability to retain mental images of objects or people not present in the room.

Playing Obstacle Course

The treasure-hunt game can grow more sophisticated as your baby does. While he is playing on the floor, place a toy he likes about three feet from him. After attracting his attention to the toy, place a pillow or a small box in front of it, making sure that your child can still see the toy. If he needs help in moving the obstacle out of the way, give him assistance; the point of the game is to help your baby see that he can set his sights on a goal, then achieve it. Another suitable learning activity for this stage is the simple game of putting objects into a receptacle — such as checkers into a plastic jar or clothespins into a box. Good play equipment includes water toys that float, stacking rings, sorting boxes, large soft blocks, plastic hammers, nesting toys and toys that open and shut.

A one-year-old demonstrates new-found skills with language by pointing to the pictures in a book when his mother calls out the names.

Increased mobility helps a child learn about spatial relationships and heightens his awareness of the many objects in a room.

Mimicking an action that he has seen many times before, the child feeds his mother. Most of what a baby learns comes through experimentation, observation and imitation.

With arms outstretched, the toddler shows that he wants to be picked up. Between the ages of eight and 12 months, children rely heavily on gestures to communicate.

Finding New Solutions

At 12 to 18 months, your child is walking boldly — though sometimes unsteadily — and jabbering all the way. She lives to experiment: What will happen if I drop this toy? Will the ball come back? Will the telephone break? Systematically, she figures out how to tilt the books to get them through the crib bars, how to hook the train cars together or how to get the macaroni out of the jar. Dauntlessly, she works toward such goals as feeding herself with a cup and spoon.

There is marked progress in her ability to remember. She recalls the way she shoved her stroller, how the lids came off the pots and pans. Now when she discovers something new, she is apt to use such memories to help her experiment appropriately: The vacuum cleaner also will roll, the top of this basket may come off, too.

A sense of her own identity is emerging. She may call herself by her own name; she can point out her head and her tummy. And though her vocabulary is limited to about 10 words, her favorite one already is "no."

Accomplishments

- Draws on past experiences and uses trial-and-error experimentation to solve problems. Her experiments become progressively more organized and systematic.

- Solves simple problems involving basic tools such as strings and handles. Is interested in how things work.

- Is able to recognize herself in a mirror by approximately 15 months of age.

- Uses memory to relate unfamiliar objects or experiences to things that she already knows.

- Begins to understand time relationships. For example, if you always take her to play in the park in the afternoon, she may go about assembling her favorite outdoor toys after her nap in preparation for the outing.

- By 18 months, may stack three blocks. Can place round pieces and, later, square pieces in an inlay puzzle.

- Shows understanding of differences in size and color, although she may not be able to name the colors.

- Will search for a toy that has disappeared from view.

- Has enough awareness of her surroundings to point to distant objects that catch her attention outdoors.

- Begins to acquire language skills and to use words in place of gestures to express her needs.

- Understands the names for many of the objects around her — chair, door, cup and so forth — though she does not yet use many of the words in speech.

- Can follow simple commands and instructions, such as "Please give the ball to me."

- Begins to learn how certain objects are meant to be used, such as a broom or a hairbrush.

Learning from Nesting Toys

When your child plays with nesting or stacking toys, let her figure them out for herself at first. Her trial-and-error approach is the best way to learn from such toys. At some point, however, praise her if she manages to use the toys for their intended purposes. At this age, she is succeeding if she stacks even two or three of the pieces, so do not be slow with congratulations. If the game seems too challenging, take away all but three of the pieces: the largest, the smallest and the one between. Similar problem-solving activities include playing with simple, two- or three-piece puzzles with knobs, and with windup toys that the child can start and stop. Some other good playthings are large, nontoxic crayons, push toys and pull toys, and large cardboard boxes for hiding in.

The toddler discovers that she can use the string to pick up her toy or to make it roll. She is beginning to focus on how things work.

The child now spends more time eating with her spoon and less time banging it on the table. This new understanding comes through observing and imitating the people around her.

Systematically turning the blocks every which way, she finally finds a way to fit them into the sorting box. Trial-and-error play complements her ability to learn through observation.

Wearing a basket as a hat, the youngster uses her recollections of something familiar and roughly the same shape to guide her in responding to something new.

Thinking Before Acting

18 TO 24 MONTHS

1 YEAR	2 YEARS	3 YEARS	4 YEARS	5 YEARS	6 YEARS

Your toddler now begins to fit the lessons of his past together like pieces of a jigsaw puzzle, to reason and form plans of action. His ever-expanding memory, now constantly in use, helps him to think before he acts. At an earlier age, out of sight was out of mind: If he dropped his bottle, it was gone and he would not think to look for it. But gradually your child has come to understand that something exists even when it is not present; moreover, he can now think of such objects on his own. And so, for example, whereas once he would have used trial and error to get at an object above his reach, at 18 to 24 months he might deliberately seek out a step stool in another room and climb on it to retrieve the object.

Watching and imitating are still the way the youngster acquires a good deal of his new knowledge. Identifying with his parents, he may wash and feed his toy animals or try to help with household chores, such as sweeping the floor. However, he also now begins to master language skills — both in understanding what is said to him and in communicating his own messages.

Accomplishments

- Can create mental images of things not in view. If asked to find an object, he may imagine the places he has seen the object in the past, then search for it at length.

- May start to plan solutions to simple problems he encounters; begins to employ reason rather than relying solely on a process of trial and error.

- Shows increased ability to remember objects, past events and experiences; begins to imitate actions, which he recalls in play and problem solving.

- Begins to be able to grasp the concept of things' happening in future time — can now comprehend the meaning of "wait a minute" and "soon."

- Can remember where many household objects belong and may seek one out when he wants it.

- Puts words together to communicate his message in simple short-cut sentences such as "Play park." Has an understanding of the personal pronouns "I," "you" and "me," as well as some action verbs and adjectives.

- By 21 months of age, can successfully place circle, square and triangle shapes in an inlay puzzle.

- Becomes increasingly more self-aware and develops an initial intuitive sense of good and bad.

- Moves and begins to dance in response to music.

Tools That Let Him Help Himself

Your toddler wants to do things for himself, and if you show him the tools that will help with a task, it will teach him a lesson about thinking ahead, without interfering with his sense of autonomy. If he is picking up his toys, for example, show him how a wagon will make the job easier. He will draw the same lesson from using a yardstick to retrieve his toys himself from under the furniture or from perching on a sturdy box to reach things up high. Suitable play equipment at this stage includes spools and beads for stringing; drums, wrist bells and other simple rhythm instruments; riding toys; balls; toy telephones; and soft clay with cookie cutters for stamping out shapes.

The newly acquired ability to create and store mental images allows the youngster to recall favorite objects, such as an ice-cream cone.

As the child's sense of a separate identity becomes more firmly established in his mind, he may recognize himself in a photograph.

The two-year-old is able to reenact familiar experiences such as songs being sung by his mother and being put down for a nap. Such imaginative games are early stirrings of pretend play.

The youngster can now imitate actions that he has observed in the past. Up till now his imitations were confined to actions that he was observing at the moment.

Using Imagination

The ability to form mental images and think on a symbolic level unleashes your child's imagination. Between the ages of two and four years, his dreams are real to him and he leads a rich fantasy life. Basing his ideas on coincidence, he may conclude that thunder causes the rain, that eyeglasses would teach him to read. He attributes life and personality to his toys and believes he can converse with animals. At the center of his own small universe, he thinks that the sun follows him when he walks, that a knife is being naughty if it cuts him. The passage of time is marked by the events of his daily routine: breakfast, lunch, nap, dinner and sleep.

Like all of the preceding stages, this period of magical thought is critical to cognitive growth. Imagination provides a safe and always-accessible arena in which to try out ideas or practice problem-solving skills.

Your youngster is eager to know all about everything, and he asks questions constantly. You may need the patience of Job to answer every who, what, where, when, how and why.

Accomplishments

- Engages in make-believe activities that gradually become more complicated and sophisticated. Begins to fantasize, exaggerate and make up stories.

- Builds roads, bridges and trains with blocks as this play becomes more symbolic.

- Is able to recall the immediate past. Remembers parts of the more distant past, although not always chronologically.

- Understands simple cause-and-effect actions — such as turning the volume dial to make the radio louder.

- Understands the concept of "whole"; puts together the two halves of a torn picture.

- By 30 months, understands the concept of "one."

- Quickly considers alternatives and makes simple decisions.

- By about 33 months, understands and remembers two-part requests, such as "Put down your toys and come in for lunch."

- By about three and a half, pairs identical pictures of objects; matches primary colors and identical shapes. Discriminates sizes; will identify the larger or smaller of two objects.

- Now understands spatial concepts such as "over," "under," "highest," "lowest," "behind."

- Understands complex sentences; by four, has about 1,500 words.

Story Play

Invite your child to act out a story as you tell it or read it from a favorite book. The more familiar the story, the better he will like the game. At first, your youngster may not want to get very involved. When you read the *Three Little Pigs,* for example, he may only be interested in huffing and puffing like the wolf who blows down the first pig's straw house. But as the child lets his imagination go, he may want to act out all of the parts in the story. Keep yourself responsive to him, changing the story if that helps his dramatization. Acting out the plot this way will help the youngster deal with the ideas in the story, and it will also help him understand that ideas can be flexibly interchanged. Good playthings for children this age include wooden blocks, pegboards, clothes for dress-up games, hand puppets, magnifying glasses, art supplies, record players and tricycles.

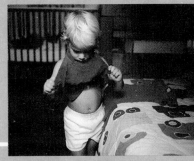

Interrupting his cycling for lunch, the youngster remembers his fun and anticipates resuming it when he has finished eating. Memory for the recent past has gradually become reliable.

By turning on the water with the faucet or lighting a room with a switch, the child grasps the notion of cause and effect — and loves to make things happen.

More practiced at thinking before he acts, the four-year-old finds it easy to make simple decisions, such as which shirt to wear. He is often sure of his opinions.

When he wants to, the child can routinely stack the graduated blocks correctly. He has progressed in his grasp of spatial relationships and mastered the distinction between large and small.

Expanding Intelligence

4 TO 6 YEARS

1 YEAR	2 YEARS	3 YEARS	4 YEARS		

The information your child has gleaned from experimenting, observing and seeking answers to her questions gives her the foundation for expanding her knowledge. After four years of age, much of her experimentation is with concepts. When she shares her thoughts about how things work or why things are the way they are, you are seeing signs that intuitive thought has become her latest method of understanding the world.

Her learning tools will continue to develop, and for years to come she will still think like a child. She still relies on appearances more than on logic; she still depends on trial and error. Making friends is easier now, though she is unlikely to consider another person's point of view. Her fantasy life is still very rich; it now focuses on acting out the roles of real-life people. She is still perfecting certain consonants, but her speech is fluent and her vocabulary exceeds 2,000 words. She loves to recite or sing rhymes and songs, and she memorizes favorite stories as you read them. With an understanding of what "future" means, she looks forward to tomorrow and new challenges.

Accomplishments

- Is familiar with the alphabet; reads simple words; writes some letters and numbers; spells her own name.

- Counts up to 20 objects; recites numbers to 30; does addition of numbers under five.

- Understands "past," "present" and "future" as concepts, but has little comprehension of history. Tells time on the hour by reading the clock. Names the days of the week by rote. Begins to understand seasons; anticipates holidays and her birthday.

- Shows forethought: for example, decides in advance what to build with the blocks. Considers implications of her actions: She will not put on the top block if she sees that it will topple the rest.

- May plan a project that takes several days to complete and then see the project through.

- Develops an intuitive sense about how the parts of a toy or a simple machine operate.

- Has increased attention span and learns more efficiently.

- Becomes less self-centered in her thinking. Develops a more realistic view of people and her surroundings.

- Can remember a three-part request, such as "Take off your coat, then get a book and come sit with me."

- Awareness of space continues to develop: talks about where she is going or has been; can make a simple mental map of the route to a familiar destination.

- Can distinguish subcategories of objects that are similar, such as coins: quarters, nickels, dimes, pennies. Matches related pictures — cup to saucer, baseball to glove.

- Pretend play turns toward more realistic themes.

Assuming Adult Roles

With her expanding insights into the world, your child enjoys acting out interpretations of what grown-ups do. To help her with a typical fantasy — playing store — collect and mark prices on suitable props such as cookies, toys, books or old magazines. Have the child sort these things into categories. Make lots of paper money and have the child count it; use buttons for the small change. Give her a muffin tin or an egg carton to fill in as a cash register. At this age, the youngster will like her pretend play to be as realistic as you can make it. Take turns buying and selling, letting the child dress up as an adult if she likes. Good play equipment includes storybooks, board games, model cars, train sets, toy typewriters and stoves, rope ladders, slides, jungle gyms, bicycles and sleds.

In the sandbox, the child now works toward a preconceived notion of what she hopes to build. She wants her constructions to be both intricate and realistic.

By the age of six, the child senses the point where stacking one block more may topple her tower. She carefully considers the placement of each new piece.

With several years of hands-on investigation behind her, she begins to have an intuitive sense of how household objects come apart and fit back together.

She can sort pennies, nickels and dimes, and she enjoys making separate stacks of the coins. Until now, they were all just "money."

4 Children with Special Needs

We have come a long way in understanding the processes that interfere with some children's ability to learn. Our progress is reflected in the words used to describe these children: Instead of negative labels such as "slow," we say "special," a word that suggests positive action.

Children may have trouble learning for many different reasons, some of them quite subtle and hard to detect. Therefore, while parents should be alert to early signs of difficulty, they must be cautious in making judgments about the source of an apparent problem. To begin with, children learn at widely varying rates, and delays in mastering specific skills are common in normal development. Such problems may well clear up without intervention as the child matures.

More long-reaching learning difficulties can be caused by a vision or hearing impairment, physical or mental handicap, chronic illness or emotional problems. Some youngsters are hindered by social and environmental factors, such as a lack of stimulation or difficulties in cultural adjustment. And still other children have a specific learning disability — an apparently brain-related kind of disorder — that interferes with their power to process information properly.

For parents who are concerned about their child's learning progress, the first step is to arrange for a comprehensive evaluation. This will usually include hearing and vision tests, a study of verbal and nonverbal mental ability, and observations of the child in learning and play environments. If the evaluation indicates a handicap, professionals can then try to match the child's disability with a special program designed to help him develop his capacities as fully as possible.

This section of the book examines the nature of specific learning disabilities, which have been the subject of much recent research, and then offers a brief overview of other physical and psychological conditions that can hinder your youngster's learning.

Learning Disabilities

To many people, the term "learning disability" means a disorder affecting school-age children — one that has been given a name reflecting classroom difficulties. For example, dyslexia is a term that has been loosely applied to a variety of reading problems, such as a tendency to see printed words reversed. The phrase dyscalculia defines trouble with math, such as the inability to understand its symbols.

But "learning disabled" is a broader term, which applies both to preschool children and to those in the classroom. It describes particular types of learning problems in which a child's achievement in one or more areas falls short of her overall intelligence or potential.

Some children, for instance, have above-average mental abilities, yet they cannot remember a simple nursery rhyme. Others excel at puzzles but have trouble understanding and following directions. There are preschoolers who can read but cannot button their clothing. Others cannot put words together into sentences, organize thoughts coherently, understand cause-and-effect relationships, coordinate some physical movements or grasp principles related to space and time.

Various attempts have been made to distinguish these sometimes mysterious conditions from other kinds of learning problems. It has been proposed that learning disabilities be defined as disorders in listening, speaking, reading, writing, reasoning or mathematical abilities. Many researchers today are taking a functional approach in studying learning disabilities, attempting to determine whether a child has a disturbance at the level of input, integration, memory or output — the steps that make up the learning process itself *(box, opposite).*

However they are described, the symptoms of such problems are distressing for parents and children alike. But aid is available, both in diagnosing learning disorders and in coping with them.

Possible causes   Efforts continue to explore the causes of learning disabilities. Experts agree that there are probably many reasons for the malfunctioning of the brain's information-processing systems. Disturbances may have occurred prenatally, during birth itself or in the early years. An expectant mother's poor diet or use of drugs, alcohol or cigarettes may restrict the blood supply and reduce oxygen to the fetal brain. Loss of oxygen can also result from a difficult delivery.

Some researchers have found a link between special learning problems and low birth weight, possibly resulting from insufficient prenatal development of portions of the brain. Malnutrition, disease or injury in the early years are suspected causes, as well. It has been suggested, too, that a genetic predisposition to specific kinds of learning disabilities exists in some families. But often a disorder cannot be explained — a condition that results in the child's inability to process certain types of information as other children do. (For reasons still unknown, learning disabilities occur five times as often in boys as in girls.)

Emotional and social effects   Seen as a total individual, a learning-disabled child probably is a lot like others her age: She does not look any different, and in many respects,

Short Circuits in the Flow of Information

Four steps take place as the brain processes information: input, integration, memory and output. A disturbance at any one of these stages can lead to a malfunction of the system.

Input, the initial step in learning, is the taking in of information — from people, objects or events in our environment. First the child sees something, hears it, smells it, touches it or tastes it with his senses; then his brain logs in the information, making basic judgments about it as part of the perceptual process. In the example mapped out below, the child has a learning disability at the input level: Although his hearing apparatus clearly receives a *z* sound, his brain misinterprets it as *d*

At the second, or integration, step, the child evaluates the information by calling on various mental processes, such as his understanding of cause and effect, or of likenesses and differences. Some young children think only concretely and have

trouble understanding words that describe categories. If such a child is asked to bring an apple, he knows what to do, but if asked for a piece of fruit, he may be confused. In this case, his integration is faulty: He perceives the direction accurately but does not understand the classifying word, "fruit."

Memory comes into play as the child places the information in his mental storage system for later use or summons information previously stored there to apply to a new situation. A problem occurs at the memory level, for example, when a child has trouble remembering names of objects or people.

Finally, there is the output stage, in which the child uses the information, either verbally or in motor activities. A child may have an output problem, for instance, if he is able to discriminate shapes accurately but cannot draw them because poor visual-motor coordination prevents him from reproducing the shapes.

INPUT

The child is asked, "What is a puzzle?" His brain improperly processes the *z* sound; he perceives "puzzle" as "puddle."

INTEGRATION

He thinks about the question he believes he has heard, evaluating the subject matter and calling on his knowledge of grammar and other verbal skills to respond.

MEMORY

To help organize a suitable answer, the child checks his memory for previously stored information about the word "puddle." He recalls having stepped in a puddle and remembers that puddles are usually caused by rain.

OUTPUT

The child's answer is well expressed: "It is the water you walk through after it rains." But it is a mystery to the listener.

she acts the same way. She is as intelligent as other children, and she has cheerful days and tearful days just as her friends do. Like any other child, she can do some things more skillfully than others and needs encouragement and reassurance to develop as fully as possible.

And yet the learning-disabled child whose problem goes unrecognized may become a lonely child if her behavior and reactions are misunderstood. She may put off potential playmates with aggressiveness or by withdrawal. Her difficulties in expressing herself may confuse other children, or they may feel uncomfortable if she exhibits impulsiveness or extreme mood shifts. Her clumsiness may invite ridicule from her peers. Moreover, having to continually face challenges beyond her capabilities may leave a learning-disabled child frustrated and confused. As she tries to participate in activities, she may become bewildered at her inability to perform. These frustrations can intensify if she enters school with her learning disability still unidentified. At this later stage, she may wonder why certain skills that seem to come easily to other children are so hard for her, and she may conclude that something is wrong with her. Once her disability is identified and her school, play and home environments become better adapted to her needs, these emotional difficulties may be resolved.

Federal assistance programs   Under federal law, a learning disability is a handicap, and a child whose learning problems fit the definition is eligible for federally financed programs similar to those available for people with other handicaps, such as the mentally retarded or the visual or hearing impaired.

Specialists stress, however, that a child who is not performing at the expected level may need further evaluation to determine whether the problem is a specific disability or simply a developmental delay that may disappear on its own in time. Because of the possibility of misdiagnosis, there has been some controversy over whether children can be accurately diagnosed before they begin school. Yet many of today's learning-disabled children can be identified by the age of five, and preschool programs for such youngsters are being established in state after state as experts realize that the greatest benefits come from the earliest possible detection.

Finding appropriate help

After a period of observing a child who is consistently demonstrating symptoms of a learning problem *(chart, pages 84-85),* parents may be ready to turn to a professional for help. Many communities and school systems offer screening programs for preschoolers, and private consultants are also available. A series of preliminary screening tests, sometimes coupled with parental interviews, can help determine whether additional tests are necessary.

Following the screening, parents may be advised to have their child further evaluated at the school or at a diagnostic center specializing in learning disabilities. There, a team of educational and psychological professionals will administer several tests and consider the youngster's performance from different viewpoints to find out which learning skills he can perform and which he finds difficult. In addition to language tests, he should be asked to perform nonverbal tasks appropriate for his age, such as skipping, drawing or buttoning his clothes. The assessment should include a medical check for visual, hearing and other physical impairments. After the tests, the evaluators will discuss with parents the kinds of facilities and services that will best meet the child's needs. Some communities have special classes for preschool children with learning disabilities; in other places, professionals are available to work individually with parents and learning-disabled children.

Programs in public schools

In many states, parents who suspect a learning problem can obtain help from their local school system even before their child has reached school age. Under current federal law, public schools must provide an evaluation without charge to school-age children, and in some states this applies to preschool youngsters as well.

Parents should keep in mind that a diagnosis is simply a tool used by professionals to determine an appropriate treatment, and it should not be used to label a child. Specialists stress the importance of regarding the learning-disabled child as a total person and of looking at what he can do as well as the skills he lacks.

Following an assessment at a diagnostic center, public schools are required to draw up with parents an Individualized Education Plan (IEP), which should be reviewed every year. Depending on the nature of his disability, the child will either remain in a regular classroom and receive individual help in a resource room, or he will join a class of other children who need special help for various reasons. Under federal law, the child must be placed in the least restrictive environment that serves his needs. The IEP designed for the child should be based on a study of his individual learning style, so that he can learn to use his strengths to make up for his weaknesses.

Parental attitudes
When they first discover that their child has a learning disability, parents may experience some of the same blows to self-esteem that the child herself feels. The immediate response is often shock, disbelief or anger, and sometimes the anger is directed toward the child. Her parents may feel that she will be less successful in the world than they had hoped, and they may resent the fact that they must now lower their expectations.

Also haunting some parents is the sense that they are somehow responsible for their child's problem. They may convince themselves that they have not spent enough time teaching the child, or they may feel genetically responsible. These feelings of guilt are often increased by the inability of professionals to pinpoint a specific cause. Uncomfortable with the situation, parents may react by blaming one another, or perhaps by denying the handicap altogether.

In other cases, parents are relieved to see a problem they sensed — but did not understand — finally diagnosed. Whatever the initial feelings, most parents ultimately identify with the child and experience vicariously the rejections and frustrations that the child suffers. And they find that adjusting their attitude and behavior to accommodate the child's difficulties is a continual process.

Support at home
No matter what their feelings, parents should remember that participation of parents and siblings is crucial to making a learning program work for a child. Parents should stay in close contact with their child's teachers and other professionals working with him. Many parents also find it helpful to seek professional guidance in choosing toys and books or in determining levels of tasks and appropriate methods of teaching or discipline.

Structured activities can help a learning-disabled child understand what he should be doing at any given moment. For example, it is important to establish regular routines at bedtime or in getting ready for school in the morning and to stick to a consistent daily schedule for meals, play, homework or watching television. Procedures should be carefully explained with simple, brief and specific directions — and in some cases, an outright demonstration of the task at hand.

Above all, the learning-disabled child needs a supportive home atmosphere to succeed. Praising his efforts, persistence and accomplishments, however small, will keep him working toward his goals and encourage him to try harder. He needs all the extra reassurance he can get to build his confidence and self-esteem. ⁘

Improving Communication

Children with learning problems often have special trouble communicating. Here are some ways that parents can help strengthen language skills:

- Try to break instructions down into separate parts and be prepared to repeat them patiently.
- Name objects and use words to describe feelings and actions as you participate in an activity with the child.
- Offer him simple but interesting experiences. Help him to remember and understand them.
- Encourage him to speak. Listen without interrupting.
- Accept gestures, drawings or pantomime until the child acquires more language skills.
- If he cannot remember words, give him multiple-choice hints or first sounds.
- Play rhyming games or sing with him.
- Face the child and speak clearly so that he can learn to speak as you do.

Early Warning Signs of Learning Problems

Many learning-disabled children can be identified at the preschool age if parents and teachers are alert to early symptoms and take note of unusual behavior or lags in skill development.

In this chart, signs associated with learning problems for children aged three to six years have been grouped into five categories: behavior; language skills; cognitive skills; preacademic skills; and motor coordination. Items in each column are presented in rough chronological order of development. It is important to note, however, that these listings are not meant to be viewed as a comprehensive development chart, nor should they be taken as signs of a problem without a thorough professional evaluation of the child.

Parents should also understand that within the wide range of these early warning signals, there is no single symptom that characterizes the learning-disabled child. Rather, symptoms usually occur together in patterns. A child with visual-spatial-motor disorders, for example, may have trouble with prewriting skills, self-help, certain games and some kinds of number problems. Similarly, if a child has difficulties with language comprehension, she will usually have trouble with reading, mathematics story problems and skills that require understanding the spoken word.

It is important to keep in mind that most children who are not learning disabled show some of these symptoms in the course of their normal development. A professional evaluation is called for if a child displays a pattern of associated symptoms persistently and frequently over a period of time.

Learning disabilities range from mild to severe, and when a child is three or four, it is difficult to predict how a handicap will affect learning later on. Early intervention, however, will prevent mislabeling a child as uncooperative, emotionally disturbed or retarded and can give her a head start in programs designed to meet her particular needs.

Behavior

These behaviors are typical of learning-disabled children. All children exhibit them from time to time, but children with learning disabilities may display some of them frequently and persistently.

● The child may seem reckless and exercise poor judgment.

● Noises and sights may easily distract him from a given task.

● He has difficulty concentrating on one activity long enough to produce satisfying results.

● The child may forget directions immediately after they are given or follow only one direction in a series.

● He may move about constantly and talk rapidly and frequently. Or the youngster may appear listless and move more slowly than other children.

● He may repeat an activity again and again until someone stops him, and then have trouble focusing on a new task.

● He may be awkward and clumsy, often spilling his milk, tripping or bumping into things.

● The child may inadvertently hit or grab instead of communicating verbally.

Language Skills

Poor language skills are key indicators of later academic difficulties and are among the most widespread and serious problems of learning-disabled children. A child may have trouble either understanding what is said or expressing her own thoughts.

● Unable to distinguish sounds, the child may confuse words she hears — such as "shop" and "chop," "cap" and "cab."

● The child may not understand prepositions of position such as "in," "on," "under" and "behind," or action words such as "jump," "run," "put" and "sit." She may not be able to follow such simple directions as, "Put the cup on the table."

● She may not enjoy having stories read to her.

● She may find it hard making sentences and may omit words or speak in single words.

● The child may have trouble remembering the words she wants to say. She may have a limited vocabulary, and she may point and gesture or use incorrect words to communicate.

Cognitive Skills

The learning-disabled child often has problems putting information together, organizing thoughts and understanding and remembering ideas.

- The child may think only concretely. He may understand the words "cat" or "table," but have trouble classifying them in general categories such as "animal" or "furniture."

- He may have trouble solving simple problems such as how to get a toy that is beyond his reach.

- He may not enjoy pretend play as much as other children do.

- The youngster may begin a task and forget how to do it in the middle of his work.

- The child may need to do a simple task or project many times before he gets it right.

- The child may have a memory problem, so that, for example, if he is shown a group of objects and then one is removed from the lot, he cannot tell which one is missing.

- He may have trouble organizing ideas or stories in order to convey them to others. Asked how to play a game, he may know the steps but have trouble ordering them correctly.

Preacademic Skills

The symptoms listed below concern early skills that are directly related to a child's eventual ability to read, write or solve mathematical problems.

- The child may not recognize likenesses and differences among letters or words.

- The child may have trouble making or reciting rhymes.

- She may be able to distinguish shapes but have trouble drawing them.

- She may have trouble learning to count.

- Because of difficulty with abstract words such as "length," "distance" and "speed," she may not be able to understand the language of mathematics.

- She may not understand the concepts of "first," "next" and "last," and she may have trouble with language associated with quantity, space and time.

- She may be confused by some math words that have more than one meaning, such as "set," "times" or "borrow."

- Because of difficulty with time-related concepts, she may show little interest in learning to read the clock.

Motor Coordination

Children with learning disabilities may demonstrate early on that they have problems managing activities that involve large- and small-muscle skills.

- The child may have trouble jumping, skipping or throwing because of difficulties associated with visual-muscle-spatial coordination.

- Right- or left-handedness may not be established and he may lack skill with either hand.

- He may have trouble continuing an action from one side of his body to the other. For example, he may switch hands to draw a straight horizontal line.

- He may have trouble judging the spatial relationship of objects to each other and to himself. This can lead to problems in dressing, riding a tricycle, going up and down stairs, and stepping over or walking under objects.

- The child may not be able to button clothes, tie or untie laces, or hold a crayon or a knife and fork securely because of eye-hand coordination problems.

- He may have problems copying shapes or doing a puzzle.

Other Obstacles to Learning

Although the information-processing disorders that are classified as learning disabilities have perhaps captured more public attention than any other kind of learning problem in recent years, parents should be aware of the many other types of physical and emotional conditions that can hinder learning in a young child. These include vision and hearing impairments, certain medical conditions, mental retardation and emotional difficulties.

As with learning disabilities, physical and emotional handicaps are best identified through a professional evaluation. And the sooner affected children begin receiving special teaching assistance — through local or federally sponsored programs — the more satisfactory their progress in learning is likely to be.

Hearing and speech disorders

Children grow up surrounded by a flow of continuous, repeated language that automatically stimulates their own language development. Yet some children, because of limited hearing, experience only silence or muffled, distorted noises. They cannot enjoy the sounds that they themselves are making, and they do not get the feedback from their own and other voices around them that is needed to correct these sounds when they come out wrong.

These hearing-impaired children often have no other obstacles to learning, but they need special help from parents and professionals in order to overcome the difficulties they have in mastering language skills. Starting at an early age, they can learn to compensate for their hearing loss with vision — through the use of sign language, finger spelling, and speech heavily cued by gestures and body language. Many children can also benefit from wearing hearing aids.

Because early detection is important, all parents, in monitoring their baby's growth and development, should keep an eye out for the behavior that reflects normal hearing development. For example, as early as two months, even when she cannot see you, your baby will turn her eyes and head in the direction of your voice. Later in the first year, she can identify the source of a sound and will turn her head and shoulders in the direction of footsteps, a ringing telephone, a voice or other familiar sounds.

If you ask an 11- to 15-month-old child to identify a favorite toy or person, she will point to or look at the object or person. By now she should also enjoy listening to all kinds of sounds and imitating them. By a year and a half, she can use her finger to point to her nose or eyes at your request. At two years old, she should be able to communicate through the use of a variety of everyday words and follow simple verbal commands without your pointing or offering other visual clues. If at any of these stages your child does not respond to sounds as you think she should, discuss your concerns with her doctor.

Formal screening of children for hearing problems is routinely done in the public schools and is often available at the preschool level. In a hearing test, the audiologist, a trained testing specialist, fits the youngster with earphones connected to a machine called an audiometer and

The Effects of Frequent Middle-Ear Infections

Middle-ear infections, which are among the most common ailments of early childhood, may be a factor in hearing and speech problems of young children who suffer frequent earaches.

The infection, known as otitis media, causes an accumulation of fluids in the middle ear that can block the sound channel and result in a mild and temporary loss of hearing. But when ear infections recur frequently in early childhood, the repeated hearing loss can interfere with language acquisition and may contribute to subsequent learning difficulties.

A child may suffer severe hearing loss if otitis media is left untreated. Therefore, experts recommend that infants and young children be regularly examined for middle-ear infections.

tests her response to a series of high- and low-pitched tones. The hearing test should be coupled with a speech and language evaluation by a professional to detect speaking problems related to faulty hearing. For example, a child may have trouble speaking clearly because she cannot monitor her voice. Her voice may be too high or low pitched, too nasal or weak, or too quiet or loud. Or she may speak too slowly or put the stress on the wrong syllables. Some speech sounds may be missing and some may be substituted for others.

Based on the results of the hearing tests, a child's impairment is categorized as mild, moderate, severe or profound. The child can also be described functionally as deaf or hard of hearing: Deaf means that hearing is so impaired that it cannot be used during the course of daily living; hard of hearing means that although the child's hearing is somewhat impaired, it is still useful. Once the problem is properly assessed, the extent and kind of help a child should receive can be determined.

Impaired vision When a child opens his eyes and looks at the world, he sees shapes, spaces and movement. This gives him a vast amount of information to take in quickly about what exists in his environment, how to move through it and manipulate it, and how others are moving through it. He notices behavior and absorbs social data by watching and paying attention to the body language and facial gestures of those around him. With his eyes closed, a child could find out a great deal of this information through hearing and touching, but it would take him a longer time.

It therefore takes longer for the vision-impaired infant's social and motor skills to develop, but the child usually catches up in the second and third years of life. The baby who has trouble seeing his parents and siblings finds it hard to understand the element of communication expressed in nonverbal cues and to imitate social behavior. He may develop his own form of nonverbal communication based on hand gestures: Although his face may be inexpressive, parents can learn to read the expression of his hands as the fingers busily scan objects presented to him or as he makes reaching gestures that announce his need for affection.

Children learn all sorts of things by exploring; if he is not visually attracted by the objects around him, the youngster's exploration of the environment is also slowed. Parents can help stimulate the interest he takes in exploration by providing a variety of sounds for him to listen to and objects to touch. But such eye-hand coordinated activities as swiping, reaching, grasping and transferring from one hand to the other hand will take more time to learn. Sitting, crawling, standing and walking will also be slowed without accurate visual feedback.

Formal evaluation of babies' vision is difficult. Parental observation of such delays in social and physical development is usually the earliest means of assessing visual difficulties.

The problems clustered under the term "vision impairment" include those of the blind child with little or no vision and the near-sighted child, who can see things close to him but not at a distance. Some children have tunnel vision, which means they can see things directly in front of them but cannot see anything on either side without turning the head. Others may have clear peripheral vision but cannot see what is just in front of them.

A child with impaired vision usually benefits from those activities that develop motor coordination and involve interaction with other children. Activities that are especially helpful to vision-impaired pre-schoolers are balancing and body movement exercises, games that involve holding hands or following directions, or sharing and singing games with finger play that combine music and words with actions. When they start school, children who have less severe vision impairments and handicaps often do well in a regular classroom that makes use of special equipment, modifications in lighting and print size, and curriculum adaptations that emphasize listening skills.

Chronic medical conditions

Many behavior and learning problems arise from metabolic disorders or orthopedic handicaps that affect a child's energy level or interfere with his processes of growth and development. These conditions are not contagious and may have no effect at all on the child's general mental abilities; children who have them often are able to participate in a regular classroom with special resources.

Malfunctions of the thyroid gland, for example, can have a great influence on a youngster's moods and on his ability to concentrate. Afflicted children may be lethargic because of excessively low levels of hormone production, or they may be restless and irritable because of too much hormone production. Similar symptoms occur with hypoglycemia, an abnormally low blood-sugar level that can be corrected through dietary changes.

Learning problems may also be present with cerebral palsy, an orthopedic handicap that interferes with muscle functioning. Some children with cerebral palsy suffer from abnormal reflexes that position their bodies into certain postures when they move, making reaching and exploring difficult. In many cases, children with cerebral palsy are of normal intelligence, but they have muscle-related speech problems that make it hard to evaluate their cognitive abilities.

The effects of other serious chronic illnesses, such as asthma, diabetes, cystic fibrosis, epilepsy or severe anemia, vary from child to child. Some children with these health problems are not usually handicapped by them in day-to-day functioning; in other cases, such illnesses require special attention on a regular basis. These children may need modified classroom activities or home- or hospital-based education programs. It is important that parents and teachers broaden the experiences of the children and help them see that the illness is only a small part of their lives.

Mental retardation

Mental retardation refers specifically to children whose intelligence and other areas of development are below normal in relation to that of their peers. These children are classified by degrees of retardation as mildly, moderately or severely retarded. Many mentally retarded children can in fact learn a great deal, even though they learn more slowly than other children.

Mildly retarded children may be good at activities involving movement but have trouble speaking, remembering, following directions and coordinating their eyes and hands. With extra help, they can learn most of the activities that take place in a preschool classroom. Moderately retarded children are physically clumsier and lag still farther behind in most areas of development. In order for them to learn, activities must be broken down into small parts and practiced one segment at a time. During the early years, the aim of a training program is to help the youngsters achieve normal developmental skills or, if this is not possible, to find ways to compensate for the lack of these skills. As children progress, some of them may move on to conventional classrooms, where the youngsters will still be provided with individual attention. Severely or profoundly retarded children can seldom be taught in a regular preschool classroom. Some never learn to speak, but they can be taught to communicate orally or with signs.

A mild or moderate retardation may not be apparent at an early age, but careful observation of a child's activities may reveal that she is slower than other children to learn new activities, complete a task or acquire social skills. Great care must be taken in evaluation, however, not to mistake physical or mental immaturity for retardation. And some children have been misdiagnosed as mentally retarded when they were simply ethnically different or economically disadvantaged.

For some retarded children, the negative expectations of parents and others provide the greatest handicap. As infants, these children need the same kind of affection and attention that other babies get: They need to be held and smiled and cooed at just like other children, even though their response to this affection may be more limited. They should have, as all children should, a program of daily activities to stimulate learning accompanied by a sense of positive expectations from other family members.

Emotional problems

For most children, occasional emotional turmoil is part of growing up. Difficult behavior may be a more stressful stage of normal development, and parents may simply have to wait for their children to grow out of fears, negativism or excessive clinging. For other children, psychological conditions are clearly blocking development and professional help is required. For example, severe anxiety can interfere with memory and concentration and reduce achievement; overly aggressive children may become a threat to other children and fail to develop social skills.

Special services are needed for the more serious types of emotional problems — including behavior that is dangerously aggressive or self-destructive, severely withdrawn or excessively hyperactive, anxious, depressed or phobic. Professionals handle most of these situations by counseling the child and by teaching parents effective methods of meeting his learning needs at home. :•

5 Foundations for Learning

During the preschool years, play is the chief means by which a child learns. It is a ticket not only to fun and adventure but also to competence and a sense of mastery over self and world. Through play, children learn about the objects, people and events in their lives; eventually they will apply the knowledge and skills thus acquired in direct interaction with the world around them.

Parents can do much to assist the process. It is not, however, a matter of telling your child how to play; children are generally their own best teachers. Instead, your contribution comes in being a resource, but providing your child with a safe, stimulating environment, tactful encouragement and interesting toys. Often the simplest playthings and activities — such as the puppet play between the mother and daughter pictured here — are the ones that are most pleasurable and, ultimately, most instructive, because they allow maximum room for the child's creative input.

In the pages that follow, you will find dozens of suggested activities, which, taken together, exercise and challenge most of the areas of growth that may begin developing from early childhood. The activities are divided into five categories and the pages are color coded: blue for activities that stimulate mental skills, such as reasoning and memory; yellow for those that foster communication; purple for artistic endeavors, such as music and make-believe; red for activities that promote the understanding of concepts in math and science; and green for physical activities — dance, swimming, group games and small- and large-muscle exercises. While a few of the projects require special toys or materials, the majority call for simple objects and playthings you will almost certainly have on hand.

The Hidden Lessons in Child's Play

Like the colorful wooden blocks children enjoy, play comes in many hues and shapes. Children may play alone or with others, quietly or noisily, with laughter or with deep concentration. But while the fundamental goal of play is fun — simply to enjoy the pleasures of the moment — indirectly it accomplishes much more.

Every kind of play forms the foundation for future learning, by providing children opportunities to develop basic skills, self-confidence and an enthusiasm for learning more. Just as a tower of blocks will stand sturdy and tall if built on a solid base, a child's success in future learning relies on a firm foundation established through early childhood play.

Consider, for example, the range of skills and concepts involved in constructing a toy railroad and village like the one illustrated below. By piecing the track together, designing a shoe-box tunnel to accommodate the train and building a station from blocks, the children practice eye-hand coordination, learn about the relative sizes of objects and engage in symbolic thinking and problem-solving exercises. They are being creative, too, making up a story to match the scene. And by talking among themselves as they play, they are developing language skills as well as learning to make decisions cooperatively.

While a free-form activity such as this one is often instructive in a number of different areas, young learners can also benefit from a range of more specially focused games, exercises and mind-stretching experiments. Reasoning, creativity and conceptualizing are all developed through certain kinds of play activities, as are communication skills and physical coordination. Once the foundation is set for these key skills, they will last a lifetime.

Children begin to learn about the world around them through play as infants — batting toys, experimenting with food, giggling at pat-a-cake. Later on, as their capabilities grow, children will amuse themselves for hours with simple, repetitive tasks, such as stacking colorful blocks and rolling balls. In the process, the youngsters are exploring such concepts as space and distance, cause and effect.

Children will also explore emotions through play, devising make-believe routines to master what is exciting, pleasurable or intimidating to them. A toddler who has been thrilled but a little frightened by a carnival pony ride, for example, may come home and pretend to ride a toy horse, picnic bench or other substitute pony over and over again, playing out the event with himself in control, until the experience no longer holds elements that upset him.

Play is a way to explore future roles, too. By two, a child will enjoy donning adult clothing and playing make-believe; a little later she will be interested in the garb of certain professions. Trying on outfits, she tries on what it would be like to be a grown-up woman, a doctor, an astronaut.

Gradually, play begins to include other children, laying the groundwork for social skills such as cooperation and sharing. Five-year-olds delight in the familiar group games — red light-green light, hopscotch and tag — activities that require them to relinquish some of their egocentric behavior in exchange for the grown-up pleasures of camaraderie.

The pages that follow contain a wide variety of activities — in five broad skill areas — for children up to six years old, with suggested appropriate ages. These are flexible recommendations: Each child learns at her own rate and will often develop ability in one area at a time, letting other areas lag behind temporarily. While not every activity will interest every child, there probably will be a few in each category that your child finds pleasurable and enriching.

Whichever activities you choose — tapping at a typewriter, growing plants from seeds, playing catch — it is important to give your child friendly, nonjudgmental support. You probably already do this quite naturally in a number of ways.

For instance, listening is a simple but very significant way to show a child you think his play is meaningful. By paying attention when he talks to you about his activities and asking questions that encourage his conversation, you are sending your child a message that you take him seriously. This confirms his belief in the value of what he is doing. When listening to your youngster, remember that children think differently from adults: They often focus on only one characteristic of an object or event, and they may have difficulty seeing points of view other than their own.

Another way to show interest and support is by joining your child in play when he wants help or a companion. Not only will you be letting him know you care about his activities enough to participate in them, you also will be revealing your own playful side, eloquently demonstrating that you think play is worthwhile. To cultivate an independent spirit in your child — and the ability to take the initiative — give him plenty of opportunity to choose what the two of you will play. Naturally, you will be the one who introduces the activities in this chapter, but he will probably develop some favorites and even suggest them on his own if you are receptive.

A secure, stimulating environment is important to your child's play. For an infant, this may mean soft toys, colorful curtains, an eye-catching mobile. A toddler needs a safe home to explore and toys that meet his increasing desire to manipulate things — a small bench for pounding pegs, for instance, or a toy on wheels to pull. Later, a box of your old clothes will spark pretend play, as will dolls, simple train sets and equipment for playing house.

Real objects often attract children more than fancy, gimmicky toys, and you may find that pots and pans, old hats and roomy cartons hold your child's attention for a much longer time than the latest mechanical-wonder toy. Most of the activities in this chapter use very simple equipment — pa-

Hints for Guiding Activities

- Introduce new activities when your child is relaxed.
- Before starting a game, you should ask yourself, "Does my child have the necessary skills?"
- Adjust activities as necessary: Make an easy one harder if the child seems bored; simplify the activity if the child seems puzzled.
- Let the child set the pace; do not push him to achieve.
- If the youngster acts restless or unhappy during an activity, stop and try it again another time.
- Keep in mind that there is no right way to approach an activity; for example, some children learn through observation, others learn through experimentation.
- To provide for mastery and a sense of success, let your child repeat activities that he is familiar with.
- Offer suggestions to your child instead of directions; emphasize fun rather than instruction.
- Show support and interest for the process of play; do not reserve hugs and smiles for results. Be sensitive to your child's mood, though; sometimes children need to try, succeed or fail without anyone watching.

per, crayo... kitchen staples, ...

Because disorder a... confusing, they can discoura... so show your child how to store mate rials when he is finished with them. But avoid creating an atmosphere in which order is more important than pleasure; children need the freedom to make messes and get dirty.

Finally, while a child should have his own private place to play, do not limit activities to one corner of the house. A spontaneous round of hide-and-seek on the living-room floor or an impromptu symphony with kitchen utensils are too much fun for either you or your child to miss.

Even at an early age, a child may show a noticeable preference and ability for one kind of play over others — drawing, for instance, or examining insects. When this happens, it is natural for parents to conclude that their child possesses a special talent in that area and perhaps to begin harboring the hope that the talent will blossom and lead to great things.

Talent, in its earliest manifestations, may be simply defined as a skill at which a child excels — and derives pleasure from performing. But the issue of childhood talent is a delicate one, requiring you to balance watching for and nurturing a particular aptitude on the one hand, with providing a range of activities and toys for your child to choose from on the other.

For example, if the musical activities in this chapter are the ones your child approaches with the greatest ease and enthusiasm, you will certainly want to give him plenty of opportunities to make and listen to music and to challenge him with advanced activities. His skill and pleasure in this one area, if allowed to grow, can bring him a great deal of satisfaction and joy, now and when he is an adult, even if he never becomes a professional musician. But you also will want to provide him with chances to build with blocks, paint a picture, learn to jump, hear a story, play charades. Childhood is a time to investigate life and its innumerable possibilities, and play is the way that children carry out the bulk of their investigations. ❖

Perception

All knowledge begins with sensory perception: No learning tools are more direct than those of sight, hearing, touch, taste and smell. From the very moment a child is born, he begins using these senses to gather information about the world around him.

When an infant drinks from his bottle, for example, he can feel its smoothness, see its shape, smell the milky aroma, taste the sweetness of its contents and hear his own sucking noises as he gulps the milk down. It is the sum of these sensory impressions that gives the baby his notion of what a bottle is all about.

The sensations bombarding a newborn seem diffuse and disorganized at first, because he, unlike an adult or older child, cannot yet separate and categorize them. But his perceptual skills grow rapidly: Within a month or so he will be able to differentiate between familiar sounds, with shapes and colors soon following. As the baby develops, he learns to organize and coordinate the input of his senses, focusing on details and relationships. For example, he associates the sight of the bottle with the easing of his hunger pangs. Gradually, the child will learn to distinguish the orange juice that is in the bottle from milk or water by its color, and to tell his own bottle from other bottles by their shapes. Throughout your child's toddler and preschool years, your youngster's ability to process sensory information will become faster, more efficient and, ultimately, more accurate.

As a parent, you first begin enhancing your child's perceptual skills by placing colorful pictures and musical toys around his crib. When language develops, you can draw his attention to details of the shapes, colors, sounds, smells, tastes and textures that surround the two of you wherever you happen to be, and later on, perhaps, you can talk about how they relate to one another.

The activities in this section are designed to help your child become aware of his five senses and how they work like built-in detectives to gather information about things around him. But you should help him see, too, that sensory stimulation can be a pleasurable end in itself — yielding, in time, a lifelong enjoyment of music, art, dance, fine food or simply the fragrance of flowers.

Matching Colors   ages 2 to 3

Colors may be one of the earliest concepts your child learns. Place four colored blocks in front of your child; two of them should be the same color. Ask her to find the two that are the same. When she does, name the color of the matched blocks. Do this for the three primary colors: red, blue and yellow. Then have the child sort the blocks into three boxes by matching the colors. This will challenge her to make careful choices while she takes a good look at colors.

Sound Tours   ages 2 to 4

Discriminating listening is important to your child's mastery of language. The first step toward this goal is to help her become aware of the sounds around her and learn to label, classify and appreciate them. You and she can take sound tours, a game she will enjoy playing over and over as she discovers there are always new and changing sounds to explore.

First, sit quietly at home with her and ask, "What sounds can we hear?" Perhaps she will notice a car passing, footsteps or a dog barking. You can ask her if the sound is near or far, high or low, loud or soft. Then you and she might walk from room to room searching for sounds such as the hum of the refrigerator, the drip of a faucet, the click of a light switch or the buzz that the vacuum cleaner makes. Outdoor sounds can be even more interesting, from the singing of birds that are hidden high in the treetops to the crunch of footsteps on dry leaves.

You can take your tour anywhere; a farm or a harbor, the zoo or places with an echo are especially fun. Call your child's attention to the patterns of sound and to the fact that rhythm is everywhere: in machines, in walking or running footsteps or in the pattern of someone sweeping. You can also use this activity to reassure her about nighttime noises: Sit with her in the dark and try to identify the sounds made by a ticking clock, a creaking door or stair, the furnace switching on or the wind blowing.

Bouncing Balloons and Balls   ages 2 to 6

In a draft-free space large enough to run in, throw a brightly colored balloon into the air so that your child can watch it move. Then let him toss it and try to tap it while it is still moving; the balloon travels through air so slowly that a child can track its motion. An older child can try tapping more than one balloon. Remember, however, never to give a young child a deflated balloon; he may choke on it.

You might also try bouncing large and small balls with your child and playing catch with him. As he becomes more adept with the ball, deliberately aim a little to his left or right, in front of him or

beyond him, to help increase his skill. With practice, he will learn to anticipate the path of the ball and get his body in the proper position ahead of time. These simple games help to sharpen your child's visual perception and develop spatial awareness and coordination.

Sniffing Games   ages 3 to 6
The next time you are baking a cake or seasoning a roast, take the time to let your child sniff each ingredient. Another way to help him experience his world through the subtle sense of smell is to call his attention to various household odors, such as fresh newsprint, soap, toothpaste, or bacon cooking. In addition, you might want to take him for a "sniff walk" in the woods or enjoy with him the backyard fragrances of honeysuckle, freshly cut grass or crushed leaves. Indoors, you can make sniffing jars by filling several jars with different aromatic substances, such as garlic, dill, bay leaves, cinnamon, chocolate or ground coffee. However, be wary of powdery substances the child might accidentally inhale. If you use liquids, such as lemon juice, vinegar or vanilla, sprinkle them on cotton balls. Encourage your child to collect samples for the jars. Let him sniff each one, with his eyes closed if he wishes, and ask him to describe what the smell makes him think of.

Sniffing a familiar smell often brings back a memory of a past event. You can encourage such memory exercises by pointing out a particular odor on a family outing and collecting a sample of the substance to bring back home. For example, when you take a walk through the woods, bring home some pine needles. Then, at some later time, take the pine needles out for your child to smell while you reminisce with him about the walk you enjoyed together. Making sensory associations in this way is a fun way to help him sharpen his memory skills.

Map Making   ages 4 to 6
Sometimes even after a child is old enough to walk to school alone, he is reluctant to do so. He may feel lost because he does not know where he is in relation to key points and lacks an overall sense of the location of his home, of the school and of the route between. You can help your child become more aware of how space is organized and of how to locate himself in relation to landmarks by drawing a floor plan of something familiar, such as the furniture in his room, or a layout of a train-track set. Then show him a street map and suggest that you and he draw a picture map of his own neighborhood. Take a walk together and let him decide what landmarks to include, such as friends' houses, the playground or the corner mailbox.

When you get home, spread a large piece of paper on the floor. Draw your own street and mark where you live, then add other streets and points of interest, labeling each item. Your child can use this map for play with toy trucks and cars or tiny dolls. You can also use the map to plan where you are going or to show where you have been, and you can expand it to show your youngster the route to school.

Encourage your child to orient himself in space when the two of you go out together by posing such questions as, "Which way is our home?" and "Where do we go to reach the store?" These ac-

tivities teach your youngster spatial awareness and help him strengthen his visual memory.

Taste Test   ages 3 to 6
Turn several lunches into a tasting game by creating a smorgasbord of interesting foods in small portions. Assemble foods that represent the basic flavors: honey, sugar and raisins for sweetness; table salt, country ham and chips for saltiness; lemon and plain yogurt for sourness; radishes for bitterness. You can also experiment with beverages.

As your child eats, talk with him about the different tastes, temperatures and textures of the various foods — the crunchy crackers and raw vegetables versus the creamy cottage cheese and peanut butter, for example. Encourage the youngster to tell you which of the foods he likes and dislikes.

Have your child hold his nose to see how important the sense of smell is to taste: He might discover that he cannot tell a raw potato from an apple. You can ask an older child to close his eyes and see if he is able to taste the differences between a potato chip, a pretzel and a salted nut or between an apple, an orange and a peach. Or you might wish to have your child join you in the kitchen as you make applesauce; let him taste the apples before and after they are cooked, and the applesauce with and without cinnamon. Be sure to caution your youngster against putting unfamiliar substances into his mouth without your supervision; you should stress that the tasting game can be played only in your presence.

Encouraging your child in these ways to explore a variety of tastes at an early age may help the youngster develop an adventurous approach to eating, as well as a lifelong appreciation of new and exotic foods.

Listening for Clues   ages 5 to 6
Hide a small object, such as a favorite toy, somewhere in a room. Have your child listen closely as you tap out the clues: When you tap softly with a spoon, the youngster is getting farther from the object; as your taps get louder, she is getting closer. This activity will give her experience in transforming information: The child will receive information in one form, the loudness of a sound, and she will need to transform it into another form, an estimate of the distance between herself and the hidden toy. The youngster's detective work becomes especially intriguing when she is far away from the object and must make choices about where to go next in her search. ∴

Creative Thinking

Simply put, to think creatively is to be fully alive, for creative thinking involves having rich and diverse ideas, the fluidity of mind to arrange and rearrange concepts, and the tenacity of spirit to carry one idea as far as it will go. This kind of thinking inspires people to concoct recipes, paint pictures or even build bridges. The ability to think creatively is an intrinsic part of childhood. Because young children are freethinking and have not yet learned to censor their thoughts with notions of "correct" and "incorrect," they naturally have many ideas of all sorts, some based on realistic premises and others on flights of fancy. A parent's most important role may be simply to respect these ideas. However, it is also possible to cultivate your child's creative thinking in other ways — offering suggestions for ways of looking at life that challenge him to think further about his toys, activities and books.

At about the age of two, when a child begins to talk in short sentences, his imagination and curiosity become evident. Before long you will probably notice how often your child asks "Why?" — when he sees a bird overhead, when the rain pours down. Soon the child has a multitude of his own ideas, devis-

ing original explanations for why things are the way they are. He makes up songs and skits, finds uses for materials you have discarded as junk, takes things apart to see how they work.

If you pay attention to your child's comments during this period, the many signs that he is already thinking creatively will be your clue that he is ready for enriching activities. He may say, for example, that sugar reminds him of snow; on a trip to the zoo, he may ask where the lion's bed is hiding. Rather than correcting this kind of thinking, try loosening your own ties to reality and having fun with your child's intriguing ideas. You might say to him, for instance, "I wonder what it would be like if snow were sugar?" or ask him how big he thinks the lion's bed would be. Such playful thinking is one of the best ways to nourish your child's imagination.

The aim of activities that ask your child to carry his natural creativity just a bit further is to fuel his zest, encouraging him to continue thinking of life in new ways. The result will be a child who will risk exploring the world from many different perspectives, a child whose mental courage adds to his sense of self-confidence.

Discovering New Uses   ages 2 to 5
Challenge your child to find new uses for common toys and objects. A handkerchief can be a flag, a spoon and pan a drumstick and drum, a paper bag a top hat. Ask your child for suggestions; he may have some you would never think of — a crayon might become a rocket; wooden puzzle pieces could be served as delicious morsels for dolls.

If your youngster is slow to respond when you ask him to imagine other uses for things, you should give him time to think and help out with open-ended suggestions such as, "Maybe this bag could be a hat. I wonder how we could do that?" But be sure to give your child the limelight: By appreciating whatever he thinks up, you encourage the youngster to think independently, and you reinforce his self-esteem.

Imaginary Travel   ages 2 to 4
On a rainy day, suggest that you and your child take a trip to the zoo in your minds. Ask your child where she would like to begin and what the animals will be doing when she gets there. To start her thinking, talk first about some of the animals, describing them with phrases that bring the image to mind — "the big, gray wrinkly elephant with its long trunk," "the funny kangaroos who hop all over their yards." After the child has visited a few animals — in her imagination — ask her which ones she would like to be. Would she like living at the zoo? This can lead to dramatic play as you and she actually become the animals. Playing zoo like this invites a child to consider how different animals behave.

Variations on a Theme   ages 2 to 4
"How many different ways can you laugh?" might be the first round in a game that involves finding different ways to perform everyday actions. Ask the child to think about different ways to get from the sofa to the chair, different ways to say "I'm hungry," different faces to make. These activities do two things: They increase self-awareness through body movement and verbal exploration, and they help the child discover that there is seldom only one way of doing something.

Creative Connections   ages 2 to 5
Now and then, set up a play area designed to encourage your child to combine objects and toys in new ways. First assemble a collection of toys and unstructured materials such as blocks, pie tins, egg cartons, crayons, clay, books and puzzles. Certainly, you do not have to use all of them at the same time; singly or in combinations, they can have many different functions. Without directing your child, let her play. She might, for example, use a

book as a wide bridge supported by two blocks, or she might make a beach out of clay, with blocks to represent nearby houses. This ability to think of different uses for objects and to use them in flexible and unconventional ways is an important part of creative thinking.

Musical Instrument Images   ages 4 to 6

Different kinds of musical instruments often call forth strong emotions and images for children as well as for adults. Play different kinds of instruments for your child and invite him to act out the way the sound makes him feel. Or ask him to match the sound to different colored paints that you have set out for him to choose from. This will help him learn to be aware of sensations gained through one avenue — a musical instrument — and to express them through other avenues, such as drama and art. Flexible self-expression is one of the goals of creative thinking.

Stepping into a Story   ages 3 to 6

Fairy tales, with their fantastic elements, make good stepping-stones to creative thinking. While you are telling a fairy tale to your child — or afterward — ask questions that encourage her to think about the characters and events from different perspectives. You might ask her, for instance, "If you were Little Red Riding Hood, what would you take in your basket to give to Grandmother?" You could even give her a roomy basket and help her gather stuffed animals and dolls to cluster inside. Or perhaps she would prefer to imagine herself as the baby bear — ask her how she would feel walking in to find Goldilocks asleep in her bed. These questions, which allow the child to put herself in the place of a character, give her a chance to see her own life in a different context. They also lay the groundwork for the capacity to empathize with others. You can ask questions about the stories, too, that focus attention on the consequences of actions and the idea that there are often different courses of action a person can choose. For instance, pause in the middle of the story of Cinderella and ask your child how she thinks the prince can find Cinderella.

What If . . . ?   ages 3 to 6

"What if you were only three inches tall? Where would you live?" "What if you were a kite? Where would you like to fly?" For young children, the phrase "what if" contains a world of playful possibilities, and children always have plenty of their own "what if 's." Add to these by asking your child questions that let his fancy soar away from reality for brief interludes.

A variation on this theme is to ask questions that contradict reality, pointing up the many aspects of the world that we take for granted. The question, "What if the sky were green?" challenges a child to think about the sky and its consistent blue or gray color — and about the variety of tones within that narrow range. Farfetched as green skies may seem, such unconventional thought processes have triggered many of the great discoveries of science and great works of art.

Create a Story   ages 3 to 6

Make up a story and at a certain point let your child finish it. If you base your story on a realistic premise, she may follow your lead and think of realistic ways to continue it. For example, you might begin: "There was a little girl who loved to climb trees. One sunny day, after she had eaten a peanut-butter sandwich while sitting in her favorite tree in her own backyard, the sky suddenly grew quite dark. . . ." Or you could begin a fantastic adventure story complete with dragons to be conquered and magic mountains to be scaled.

If you substitute your child's name for the heroine of the tale, she may be inspired to imagine what kinds of supernatural powers she would like to possess. To keep the story going, or if your youngster gets stuck, you can take a turn at spinning the plot. This approach increases the child's tolerance for change, since she must adapt to your additions to the story.

I'm Thinking of Something . . .   ages 4 to 6

Think of a simple, common object for the child to guess and open the game with, "I'm thinking of something white and cold. What is it?" If the child guesses snow, tell him that snow is one thing it could be. Then ask him what it might be if it were white and cold and you could eat it. Now he might offer a piece of cauliflower as a guess. Again, let him know that is a good guess, but keep the game going by adding another quality such as sweetness. Thinking of all the different things in the world that are white and of their many different qualities is both entertaining and mind stretching. In addition, it can teach the child to carry an idea a long way. ⋰

Memory and Reasoning

A child's ability to solve problems and take a logical approach to life is based on the mental powers of memory and reasoning. Memory — the capacity to store and recall information — starts to develop around the middle of a baby's first year. As his memory grows and as he encounters situations requiring logical thinking, the child learns to reason: to sort and classify things, to understand how past or present events relate to one another and to draw conclusions from his observations and memories. During the early years, a child's "how" and "why" questions are signs of a reasoning mind at work.

A child is ready to put memory and reasoning to use in solving very simple problems — such as nesting and stacking objects — around the end of his first year. By the age of three he is able to work out problems that involve remembering what he has learned and keeping track of what he is doing at present — fitting the pieces of a familiar puzzle together, for instance. A five-year-old can remember information that is not specifically related to the problem at hand: If a large ball has lodged in a tree, he might be able to figure out a way to get it down with an unrelated object, such as a broom.

Be alert for indications that your child is ready to tackle such problems and stand ready to offer guidance — but do not step in with a solution right away. Lead him gently through the steps that are involved in solving all problems, large or small: first identify the problem, then consider possible solutions and finally, decide what to do. For example, when your three-year-old expresses frustration with a tower of blocks that keeps toppling, you might say, "You seem to be having trouble. Let's see if we can figure out what the problem is." Then show him how to think about the block tower logically — considering different ways of stacking the blocks, for instance — in order to come up with possible solutions. Remind him that he might have to try several solutions before he finds one that works well. The aim in helping your child develop these basic mental skills is to guide him to autonomy; through solving their own problems, children feel a sense of accomplishment and pride. They learn to be flexible thinkers adept at considering a variety of options. They learn as well to trust their own judgment, as they secure the confidence necessary to tackle the next problem.

Following Directions   ages 2 to 6
You can begin to teach your child to remember and follow directions — a skill she will need throughout her life — if you keep your requests simple and avoid overloading her with too many instructions at one time. A two-year-old may have trouble remembering directions that require more than one or two actions, so start by asking her simply to pick up a toy and put it on the table. Or, you might ask her to sit down in her chair and look at her favorite book. As she grows and demonstrates her understanding of such simple directions as these, gradually increase the number of steps or actions you ask her to perform. A somewhat more complicated set of directions might involve, for instance, asking the child to take a ball out of the closet, to shut the closet door and then to throw the ball to the dog in the backyard. Exercises such as these, which can be casually incorporated into the day, help a child get ready for listening at school as well as challenge her to remember several things at once.

What's Next?   ages 3 to 4
A child needs plenty of opportunities to think ahead and to predict what is going to happen. Since children also like to make things happen, you can combine the two. For instance, ask your child what he thinks will happen to the bath water if you put in a capful of bath bubbles. After he has a chance to imagine the outcome, let him pour in the soap and watch as the water foams.

Later, in preparing him to go outside, try another kind of thinking-ahead activity. Ask him to figure out what comes next in a sequence of events — in this case, dressing warmly for a snowy day. You might say, "You have put on your hat, your jacket, your mittens and your heavy socks. What comes next?" If the child does not guess that his boots are next, give him a hint: Rub his

toes or ask what goes on feet after socks. The ability to think ahead and to remember a sequence of events from the past are early steps in the process of reasoning, which often involves forming conclusions from known facts.

Memory Book   ages 3 to 6
Start a scrapbook for saving and recalling special memories; it can include photos, souvenirs and thoughts your child dictates for you to record. After a trip to the zoo, a ride on the train, or a family gathering, for example, collect the memorabilia from the event — photos, postcards, a train-ticket stub. Talk them over with your child and then arrange them in the scrapbook. A few days later, look at this section of the memory book and encour-

age your child to remember the event as she leafs through the pages. Limit the number of events in the book to those that are important to the child, so she knows it is her own special book. As she becomes familiar with it, she may ask to record an event on her own. Set aside quiet times for you to look through the whole book together, enjoying happy memories. This teaches your child to know the pleasures of remembering in addition to expanding her ability to recall the past.

What's Different?   ages 3 to 6

Start this activity by placing three or four related objects on a table. Organize the objects around a particular theme — kitchen utensils, for example. Show your child the objects and ask him to look at them carefully, naming them one by one. Then have him turn around or cover his eyes for a moment while you remove one of the objects. When he looks back at the table, ask him to guess which object you have removed. As a variation, you can introduce a new object to the collection, one that does not fit the theme — a Teddy bear, perhaps. This time, have your child pick out which object does not belong in the group. If he finds this difficult, help him to think about it logically: Mention that all the items that were on the table at first are used for eating or cooking. Then ask him again if he knows which object was added and does not belong with the others.

Once your child has mastered these two versions, go a step further by lining up three or four similar items in a particular order on the table. Have him study the arrangement and suggest that he say the names for the objects out loud, to imprint them in his memory in the proper order. Then, have him close his eyes and change the location of one object. Ask the child to open his eyes and put things back in the original order. These activities exercise your child's visual memory and his short-term recall. They also teach him how to use the technique of associating similar things as a memory aid.

Analogies   ages 4 to 6

Analogies, relationships between pairs of words or concepts, can be an entertaining way to kindle logical, analytic thinking in a youngster. Using toys to illustrate each analogy encourages your child to fill in the blank verbally. For instance, show the child a toy cow and barn, and tell him that the cow's home is the barn. Then show the youngster a bird and ask him to name the bird's home. As you speak, emphasize the word — home, in this case — that reveals the relationship between the pair of words. (The adult form of this analogy would be: "Cow is to barn as bird is to nest.") Try other themes such as animal sounds, relative size or

textures. Each time you play you will be helping your child learn to reason through recognizing relationships.

Twenty Questions   ages 5 to 6

Here is a mind-stretching game to play with the family or in a play group. Divide the players into two groups, with at least one adult and one child on each team. First, one team decides on a word that the other team will try to guess — "peach," for instance. Then, a member of the first team says to the guessing team: "I am thinking of a fruit." By asking questions that can be answered by "yes" or "no," the guessing team tries to discover what the fruit is. If the word is still a mystery to the guessing team after 20 questions have been asked, the team must make a final guess. Then the other team takes its turn at guessing a word.

This game encourages logical thinking, because mere guesswork seldom yields an answer. The adult on the team trying to guess the answer may need to run through the logic out loud: "Let's see, we know it's round, you can eat it, it tastes good and it isn't an apple. But it is a fruit. What else could it be?" Twenty questions also helps children learn how to classify objects into groups such as fruits, to think about similarities and differences and to reach conclusions by narrowing the field of possibilities.

Sample questions about a peach:
I am thinking of a fruit.
Q. Is it round?
A. Yes.
Q. Is it crispy?
A. No.
Q. Is it fuzzy on the outside?
A. Yes.
Q. Is it a peach?
A. Yes!

Mazes   ages 3 to 6

Even before your child can read she will enjoy making choices that lead her through a maze. You can draw your own mazes, starting with a simple path that runs from start to finish with no obstructions. If your child does not yet handle a crayon or pencil easily, have her trace the path with a finger. As she gets faster at threading through the maze, create more complex designs by adding side roads and dead ends. Giving the maze a theme will make it more fun. You might put a picture of an ice cream cone at the end and call the maze "Find Me Before I Melt." Mazes require judgment and reasoning, particularly the ability to look ahead and visualize a solution. ⁘

Language

Language is the most fundamental of communication tools, the key that unlocks the door to personal expression. In time, your child will use language to master reading and writing, to acquire knowledge, to think through problems and arrive at solutions. Through language she will be able to communicate her ideas and feelings, and to understand and be understood by others.

Youngsters learn to speak without any formal instruction, and they progress in natural stages. Babbling and cooing at six months, your child will form her first words as she nears her first birthday and may speak in two-word sentences by her second. When she realizes that everything has a name, her vocabulary will grow at a phenomenal rate — from about 20 words at 18 months to almost 300 words at the age of two and 1,500 words by the time she is four. Now she may begin to ask "how" and "why" questions, listen intently to the answers and express two or more ideas in a single sentence. And when she is six, she will be chattering away fluently.

Parents should remember, of course, that children advance at different rates according to their experience and environ-ment. But if you talk and respond to her, let her hear others talk and generally surround her with language, she will learn eagerly and rapidly. Talk to your baby from birth; she will delight in the musical sounds of your speech. As she grows older, introduce her to new words and help her recognize the rhythms and patterns of language by playing word games, singing songs, reciting nursery rhymes, telling jokes and read-ing stories. Keep your conversations throughout the day spontaneous, and be sure to respect your child's wishes when she does not feel like talking.

In the beginning, it is more important to concentrate on communication than correctness. If you use good grammar, your child will pick it up eventually. If she says, "Go bye-bye?" you can respond, "You would like to go out? What a good idea. Where shall we go?" Your answer tells her that you understood, offers a more mature version of the same idea, and encourages her to express herself further. Your goal is simply to help your youngster feel comfortable as she begins to experiment with words, and to discover the fun and ex-citement of language.

Changing Voices   ages 1 to 4
By changing the sound of your voice, you can help teach your child how to control her own voice by altering tone and volume. The youngster will be fascinated by the different sounds as you speak to her through the cardboard tube from an empty roll of paper towels or talk into a paper cup. Try singing your child's name, first in a high, shrill voice, and then in a low, rumbling voice. Whispering into your child's ear is fun because it tickles and, at the same time, makes you feel close to each other. You can play this voice game with any word or phrase that the child is familiar with, such as "Are you my little sweetheart?" You should en-courage your youngster to join in so that she can start exploring the range of her own voice.

Say and Play   ages 1 to 3
You can use physical play — such as running, tumbling and roll-ing around — to introduce your youngster to the words that de-scribe what she is doing and to the words that name the different parts of her body. As your child is running around, run with her and say, "We're running around and around," or if she is crawl-ing, "Now we're crawling all over the floor." Try suggesting things that the two of you can do with various parts of your bod-ies, such as "Let's wave our hands in the air" or "Can you touch your toes like this?" or "Let's tug at our ears." Your child may need help at first, but she will soon learn to associate the meaning with the words.

Moving On, In, Around, Under   ages 2 to 4

Prepositions are important words for your youngster to learn early in life because they will help her see objects in relation to one another. You can use a favorite toy or stuffed animal to teach her such words as "on," "in," "around," "under" and "behind." Have her take her Teddy bear, for example, and help her move it from place to place, saying, "Let's put Teddy in his bed. Oh, he wants to hide. Can you put him behind the toy box? Now, he wants to stand on top of it and jump down." Each time, emphasize the action with your voice. Later, you can change the game by asking her to perform the actions herself — sitting on the bed, walking around the chair, crawling under the table. Prepositions are basic linking words and learning them is a primary step in language development

What's in the Picture?   ages 3 to 4

Cut out some interesting pictures from an old magazine. Choose pictures that are colorful and have lots of detail, then paste them on pieces of cardboard. Place three or four cards in front of your youngster and ask her to describe everything she sees in the pictures. Give her plenty of time to study the scene and encourage her to use all the words she knows to talk about the objects — their size, shape, color and position or action.

You can help by gently inquiring, "What is the dog in the picture doing?" or "Are all the trees the same size?" You and your child can play this game just about anywhere — indoors or out, with a poster on her bedroom wall, or even with the window display in a store. Your youngster will increase her powers of observation and strengthen her descriptive skills, both of which are essential to reasoning and evaluating.

Making Conversation   ages 3 to 6

You can enhance your youngster's verbal skills in a simple and natural fashion by taking a couple of pretend or toy telephones and talking back and forth on them, just as she has seen you do hundreds of times using the real telephone. Ask her what she did today, how her doll is feeling, what she had for lunch, what the weather is like outside. Encourage your child to ask you questions and to think about what is happening in your day. This will give her an early lesson in the social graces — learning to listen and make conversation.

Exploring Feelings   ages 3 to 6

The characters in a story can help you to explore emotions with your child. As you read to her — from the story of the "Three Little Pigs," for example — pause now and then to ask questions about a character's feelings: "Do you think that the little pig is scared of the wolf?" "How did the wolf feel when he couldn't blow the house down?" "Was he angry?" You might encourage her to think about and name the feeling by saying, "That pig built such a strong house that the wolf couldn't blow it down, no matter how hard he tried. How do you think that makes the pig feel?" When your child responds, follow up on her answer with a statement such as, "I think you're right. That little pig must feel very proud of himself."

You can also ask her how she would feel in a similar situation. For an older child, you can change the questions a little and ask her how she would feel if "the wolf really did manage to blow the house down." Your child will not only think about feelings, but will develop her language abilities as she searches for words with which to express her emotions.

Silly Questions   ages 3 to 6

This game will encourage your youngster to listen intently and use her reasoning skills. Tell her that you and she are going to play a new question-and-answer game. Explain that some of the questions you are about to ask will make sense but that others will sound very silly. Her job is to listen carefully and answer with a "yes" for those questions that make sense and a "no" for those that are silly. Then pose such questions as, "Can trees eat ice cream?" "Can birds fly?" "Do bunny rabbits go to school?" "Does a doggie have a shaggy coat?" Later, as your youngster's experience and reasoning powers grow, you can include trick questions — sensible questions that sound silly at first but make metaphorical sense, such as, "Do trees drink water?" or "Can cars and trucks blink their eyes?"

Rhyming Games   ages 4 to 6

Rhyming games can help teach your child to listen carefully to word sounds and to enjoy the cadence of language. Recognizing word endings will also help her gain reading and spelling skills. You can start by reciting a nursery rhyme, such as "Twinkle, Twinkle, Little Star," and then point out the words that rhyme: " 'Star' and 'are' sound alike — they rhyme." After a bit, you can vary the game by telling her, "Now I'm going to say some more words that rhyme, but one word won't rhyme with the others. When you hear it, say 'stop.' " For example, you might say, "Shoe, blue, you, tree." If at first she does not hear the nonrhyming word, patiently repeat the words.

You can make the game more interesting by putting the nonrhyming words alternately at the beginning, middle or end of the phrase. You can play the game with different activities throughout the day, rhyming words with nap, eat, toy, run and so forth. And you can expand the game for an older child by suggesting that she fill in the rhyming word and act it out. Once the youngster gets the hang of it, you can ask her to make up rhymes of her own and act them out for you.

Reading and Discussing   ages 4 to 6

As you read to your child, you can help him enhance his listening and speaking abilities by talking about the story. When you start a new book, point to the cover and ask him what he thinks the story might be about. While reading it, pause and ask what he imagines will happen next. At the end of the story, you can ask questions about it, such as "What was your favorite part of the story?" and "What do you suppose made those stepsisters so mean?" As your youngster gets older, you can ask him to summarize the story and to tell you what it was mainly about. Recognizing the main point is an important but difficult skill, one that takes time and experience to develop. ⁂

Reading

A child can begin developing the fundamental skills of reading in the years before she goes to school. A working vocabulary of spoken words and a familiarity with the appearance and sounds of the alphabet learned at home, for example, will help a child progress naturally into reading. As a parent, you can help your child acquire these skills by talking to her often and by providing toys and activities that make her aware of the alphabet. Just as important, you can show your child that reading is relaxing and enjoyable by reading to her often.

Even a baby benefits from an early introduction to books and reading. While an infant likes to finger and mouth her picture books, a one-year-old enjoys looking at the illustrations and having you turn the pages with her, pointing out colorful objects and animals and people. Toddlers between the ages of one and two are inclined to listen more attentively to stories and to remember a few words from them, but they lose interest quickly and find it hard to sit still for long periods of time. The child's attention span and patience soon increase, however, and children of three to five years take pleasure in hearing relatively long tales, requesting their fa-

vorites over and over again, virtually memorizing them and retelling the stories in their own words.

To know when your child is ready for prereading activities, look for clues in her verbal aptitude and interest. This may consist of a large vocabulary and an ability to speak clearly, demonstrating that she is able to distinguish the sounds of different letters. As she matures, her curiosity about your reading and about words she sees around her grows; she may ask questions about what you are doing, about signs and print on packages, and about how to spell words she hears often. Casually follow up on such queries; for example, once you have shown her how her name is spelled, occasionally point out other places where some of the same letters appear.

During your child's progress toward reading, the goal is to help her enjoy the enterprise, without pressuring her. The activities on these pages are playful ways of focusing your youngster's attention on words, sounds and letters. From contact with the elements of reading — and from frequent, pleasurable experiences with books — she will derive the confidence and enthusiasm that make reading fun.

the illustrations. Begin looking through the book with your child and, while pointing to one of the illustrations — an orange, for instance — say the word very clearly. Then pick up the real orange and show it to her, repeating the name of the fruit. If she has begun to talk, encourage her to try to say the word.

Incorporate this activity into some of your reading times, and soon your youngster will learn that pictures depict the things around her and that these things have names. This concept, which involves a rudimentary understanding of symbols, is an important one for the child to be exposed to before she begins learning to read. In addition, any time that you and your youngster enjoy reading together, the child's desire to read is sparked just a little bit more.

Name Game   ages 2 to 4
Perhaps the most important word to your child is his own name. Spelling it out when you call him is one playful way to demonstrate that letters make up words and to teach him to recognize the particular letters in his own name. You can do this spontaneously at different times during the day. For instance, as you call your child to dinner or ask him to play a game, spell, then say his name. After a while, when he has begun to associate his name with the way the letters sound, show him how they look by writing them on paper in large print. Later, to help your youngster distinguish the letters of his name from others, point them out on signs and in books.

When your child notices that the letters of his name appear all around him, his curiosity about other letters will be triggered; this is your chance to introduce him to the rest of the alphabet. Letter recognition and mastery of the alphabet are, obviously, essential prerequisites to learning to read.

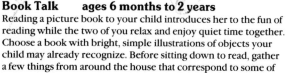

Book Talk   ages 6 months to 2 years
Reading a picture book to your child introduces her to the fun of reading while the two of you relax and enjoy quiet time together. Choose a book with bright, simple illustrations of objects your child may already recognize. Before sitting down to read, gather a few things from around the house that correspond to some of

word that begins with a different sound. This activity makes a good diversion when books are not available or while waiting in a long line or taking a car trip, and it helps the child learn to distinguish one letter from another simply by listening.

Matching Letters   ages 4 to 6
To set up this activity, which involves matching like letters of the alphabet, print several capital letters on a large piece of paper or cardboard. Leave a sizable space next to each character and attach a few pieces of double-sided tape in this space. Hang the poster low on the wall, where your youngster can reach it easily. Then write the identical letters on index cards or on smaller pieces of cardboard. Ask your child to stick each card next to the letter on the poster that matches it. Older children can play this game with short words. And for a child who can read and understand some words, you can substitute pictures for the letters on the poster, then write the names for the pictured items on cards. Ask your child to match the word cards with the illustrations on the poster. You can point out to your child that she is making a sign, like the signs she sees alongside the road or in front of a store. The activity enhances the youngster's ability to recognize letters and words and — when done with pictures — emphasizes that words are symbols.

Keyboarding   ages 4 to 6
Typewriters and computer keyboards capture a preschooler's attention as few devices can, and they are especially fun for word play with children who do not yet have the manual dexterity to write well-formed letters. The keyboard allows them to play with letters and words without becoming frustrated by an inability to hold and use a writing implement skillfully. If you use a typewriter, be sure your child can depress the keys easily.

Explain at the outset that the machine is delicate. Ask the child to treat it carefully, and show her how to hit only one key at a time. Before turning the machine over to your child, press the shift-lock key so the keyboard will produce only capital letters; this will prevent confusion caused by one key's being responsible for two different kinds of letters. When your child types a letter, point out the resemblance between it and the same letter on the keyboard. You can also have one of the child's large-print books on hand to show her that letter in the book. Ask her to copy some of the words from the book. If your youngster already knows how to spell some words, you can encourage her to type these, too. But do not be disappointed if the child gets the most pleasure from just tapping randomly on the keys; this will focus attention on letters just as well as more structured typing. ⁖

Acting Out Words   ages 3 to 6
A simple form of charades can improve your preschooler's comprehension of words. First, print action verbs such as "jump," "skip," "run" and "fall" on index cards, one action word per card. Then gather a few members of the family together and ask the first player to pick a card and act out the word written on it until someone guesses what the word is. The player who guesses correctly keeps the card; if no one guesses the correct word, the card goes to the bottom of the stack. Then the next player takes her turn drawing a card and acting out the word. The game is over when all the cards have been won; the winner is the person with the most cards. You can adapt this game for younger children by adding a picture of the activity above each word as a clue.

Name Tags   ages 3 to 6
Once your child knows the alphabet, you can label objects in his bedroom to help him recognize common words. To make name tags, print words in large, clear letters on index cards, then tape the cards to the appropriate objects. Begin with highly visible, familiar items such as his bed, a table or a chair. For the older child who already recognizes words for these objects, try labeling the curtains, a picture or a toy truck. As you attach the tag to the item, be sure to pronounce the word. Mention it at other times as well. Later, make a duplicate of one of the cards and see if your child knows what it says. If he does not, invite him to search around the room until he finds its mate.

Letter Sounds   ages 3 to 6
Children need to know that letters are symbols for sounds, and they must learn to associate the appropriate sound with individual letters. To help your child with this skill, first decide on a certain letter that the two of you will hunt for in a book. In the beginning, choose letters that are easy for the child to hear and say, such as *B, D* and *T;* you may notice others that are particular to your child. Then, while you are reading a book with large print to your child, emphasize all the words that begin with that sound. Ask him to repeat the opening sound with you. For instance, point out that the word "ball" begins with a *ba* sound and ask him to repeat the sound. Point to the letter as you and he say the sound. Then, ask him to find some other words on the page or in the book that begin with *b.* You can also try a similar activity but without the book. Say words in groups of three — "book," "bat," "rug," for example — and ask your child to pick out the

Writing

Writing, a skill that adults take for granted, actually requires several fairly sophisticated abilities. Before a child can form letters, he must have the manual dexterity to hold and make strokes with a writing implement, and he must have sufficient eye-hand coordination to look at a letter and reproduce it. Just as important, he needs an idea of how printed language is used for communication — something he acquires in large part through watching adults read and write and by being read to himself. While children usually do not learn formal writing until the first grade, there are many activities that help them develop the preliminary skills. Early endeavors with crayons give a child practice in holding a writing tool, strengthen hands and fingers, develop muscle control and train the hand to reproduce what the eye sees. Even tasks such as fastening buttons and tying shoes contribute to small-muscle strength and eye-hand coordination.

You will naturally want to choose activities that are in step with your child's emerging capabilities. A 10-month-old may well show eager interest in the pen you are using, but he is not quite ready to grip it as a writing tool. In another few months, though, he will happily clutch a fat crayon and scratch designs wherever you let him. These first scribbles gradually evolve into more controlled strokes until, by the age of three, he may be able to copy very simple shapes: the letter *t*, perhaps, or a circle. At four or five, a child can usually draw a recognizable picture and probably print his name.

Be alert to signals from your child that he is ready to experiment with marker and paper or is ready for more challenging prewriting activities. A one-year-old who manipulates small toys easily can be given a water-soluble felt-tip marker and shown how to move it over a big sheet of paper to make squiggles. And when your four-year-old expresses curiosity as you draw up a grocery list, ask him if he would like to help. Although his words may look nothing like yours, the general form of his scrawl will probably resemble writing.

There is no need for a preschooler to produce perfectly formed letters and complete words. Rather, the purpose of early writing activities is to establish the physical coordination and enduring enthusiasm that will make learning to write in school easy and enjoyable.

Scribble-Scrabble   18 months to 3 years
To make scribbling easier for your child, tape two large pieces of paper to a table. Give the child a felt-tip marker with bright, washable, nontoxic ink and show him how to move the marker across the paper to make designs. Casually point out how the child's arm moves as he draws and demonstrate, copying his marks, with your own arm. With a little practice, he will gain control and be able to make more exact lines and even to repeat what he has drawn. Repetition should be encouraged, since it is part of learning fine-motor control. There is no need at this point, however, for the child's work to be precise; instead, use scribbling for creativity and fun. Along the way, your youngster will be gaining muscle control and eye-hand coordination, as well as getting accustomed to holding a writing implement and making basic strokes with it.

Chalk Silhouettes   ages 2 to 3
Lay a large chalkboard flat on a low table. Have your child sit at the table — this approximates the correct writing posture better than standing — and offer her colored chalk and a number of items with simple shapes to trace around. Plastic cups, blocks, cookie cutters in geometric shapes, leaves and shells are all easy to outline; your youngster might enjoy tracing around her own hand, too. Show her how to hold the chalk like a pencil, with a relaxed grip and the index finger on top. Demonstrate how to outline an object on the chalkboard, using a wet finger first, then chalk. Chalk is especially fun to draw with and is easily erased, so the youngster can experiment with what she thinks looks right and what does not. Erasing and redrawing — the act of repetition — exercises her fine-motor control and reinforces her experience with the different shapes of objects.

Different Strokes   ages 2 to 4 years
Drawing directly with fingers instead of an implement is often easier for a small child. With your child's assistance, spread shaving cream, cornmeal or finger paint on a large tray. Finger paint can be spread thinly; cornmeal and shaving cream should be about one quarter of an inch thick. Using your index finger, demonstrate to your child how to draw a line in the substance. Ask your child to do the same. Then draw a second line, crossing the first, and suggest that the child do this, too. Try *x's*, pluses, curves and circles, introducing the names of the figures the two of you are making. It does not matter if the circles are not round and fully closed or if the lines are wavy and crooked; your child is gaining firsthand experience in what shapes look like and what they are called, two important precursors to learning to write.

Tracing Pictures and Words   ages 3 to 6

Your child is likely to have discovered tracing already in an effort to copy an interesting picture. Taken one step further, tracing can be used to give him practice in shaping letters and geometric designs. First gather some bold, colorful graphics from magazine advertisements and look through them with your child, talking about the different designs. Ask him if he would like to draw something like them and, if he has not learned how to trace yet, explain that this is easily accomplished by laying a thin piece of paper over the original and tracing the outline. Then tape tracing paper or onionskin typing paper to the pictures the child has chosen and show him how to trace around the edges with a marker or pencil. Pictures with clear, heavy outlines and sharply contrasting backgrounds will be easier to trace. As your child traces, be sure to mention some of the shapes he is drawing. This will call his attention to the wide variety of shapes he can make — circles, squares, ovals, triangles.

You and your youngster can also do this tracing activity with an alphabet book that has large letters; talk to your child about the different letters and the shapes involved in them. For a young child, tracing letters is easier and less frustrating than copying them, and the activity still gives the youngster the opportunity to observe and make the characters.

Making Letters from Dough   ages 3 to 6

For this exercise you will need nontoxic molding clay or homemade dough (below). Break the dough or clay into manageable chunks that fit easily into the child's hand. With your child, shape each chunk into a rope, then form letters with the ropes. You and she can combine the letters into short, familiar words, such as her name. This play with three-dimensional letters gives her a chance to work with the alphabet even before she can write it. And molding the clay and dough is good for strengthening hand muscles and improving manual dexterity.

Recipe for homemade dough: Mix two cups flour, one cup salt and two tablespoons cream of tartar in a pot. Add one tablespoon oil and two cups water and stir over medium heat until the mixture is thick and blended. Cool the dough until it can be handled, then knead out any existing lumps in it.

Dot-to-Dot   ages 3 to 6

Using dots, outline a letter of your child's name or another simple shape on a piece of paper and ask the youngster to connect the dots with a marker or crayon; demonstrate how, if necessary.

To make the activity more intriguing, you can turn it into a mystery: Ask the child what she thinks is going to emerge on the paper and then share her surprise when something recognizable appears. Give the child several opportunities to complete a letter, especially any that are difficult for her. And if you later increase the challenge by creating whole words in dots, for contrast you might want to offer your child a marker of a different color for each letter in a word.

Older children can do a similar connect-the-dots activity with yarn and heavy cardboard. Using a hole punch or scissors, punch large holes through the cardboard in the pattern of letters. Give the child yarn to thread through the holes; a little dried glue or nail polish on the end of the yarn makes a firm tip that will pass through the holes easily. Both variations of this dot-to-dot activity give children practice forming and recognizing letters — with the added element of suspense.

Writing and Mailing a Letter   ages 3 to 6

Suggest to your child that he write a letter to a relative. The writing can be the youngster's own scrawls and first attempts at shaping letters, or it can be a joint effort, in which he dictates and you do the actual writing. Offer suggestions for what he might say, for example, "We baked a chocolate cake today." Before you seal the letter in an envelope, enclose a short note asking the recipient to respond. As you address the envelope, point out to your youngster that this shows the mail carrier where the person who is getting the letter lives. You can also explain to the child that the stamp pays for the letter to be delivered. Make a special project of mailing the letter; let your child hand it to the mail carrier or put it in the mailbox. If you have an instant-film camera, take a picture of the youngster mailing the letter so that he can refer to it as a reminder during the days he is waiting for a reply — and on the day a return letter comes.

Alphabet Cards   ages 3 to 6

Write the alphabet on colored index cards, one big letter to a card. Spread five or six cards on a table and give your youngster some blank cards and a water-soluble felt-tip marker. Now ask the child to copy the letters he sees onto his blank cards — again, one per card. Young children often have trouble copying from a distance, so be sure the original cards are close to where the child is working. This activity will familiarize him with the alphabet and give him practice in writing without the necessity of arranging letters on a page. It also allows the youngster to concentrate on one letter at a time. ❖

Music

Music has an irresistible attraction for children. An infant scarcely two months old may stop squirming at the sound of music, enraptured by what she hears. A nine-month-old will sometimes start rocking back and forth or waving her arms when a lively tune comes on the radio. A youngster of two will sing along, perhaps not coming very close to the melody or the words, but thrilled nonetheless at her own capacity to make music. With this kind of built-in motivation, no extraordinary effort is required to foster your youngster's musical development.

The first step, starting as soon as your child is born, is to see that there is music in the home. This does not mean inviting a string quartet to play in your living room. Just turn on the radio or play records. Begin with music you yourself enjoy — whether Beethoven or the Beatles — and let your youngster sense your enthusiasm. Sing to her. Do not hesitate because you feel you cannot sing. Your three-month-old will not criticize your performance; she will be delighted to hear the music you make with your voice, and before long she will try to do the same. You may think that you do not know any songs. But what about "Mary Had a Little Lamb," "Three Blind Mice" or "Old MacDonald"? With a little effort you can learn half a dozen more children's standards.

Programs of formal musical instruction are available for children as young as three. One, the Suzuki method, teaches students to play tunes from memory on miniviolins and other scaled-down instruments. Others, among them the Dalcroze, Kodály and Orff methods, concentrate on body movement, voice training and improvisation with special xylophones and glockenspiels. Yet with no formal instruction and just a little encouragement, your six-year-old can learn to beat time to a tune, to sing simple songs more or less on key, to make appropriate use of such instruments as a triangle and tambourine, and to distinguish the sounds of a few orchestral instruments. In addition, her musical experience will have lengthened her attention span and sharpened her listening ability. Above all, the youngster will have learned the joy that music can give, and she will have embarked on a continuing musical education that will add another dimension to her life.

Mood Music   birth to 2 years
Music surely does have charms to soothe the savage breast, including that of the youngest infant. Lullabies are not merely a quaint tradition; they work wonders to calm a cranky or restless baby. Try holding him close with his head on your shoulder and singing or humming softly to him as you sway back and forth. Or play a quiet record that he has responded to in the past. The effect often is magical, and the association of music with such warm, comforting moments can only enhance its long-term appeal. Music is also useful in changing a baby's mood to suit a new situation. If he is bouncy and rambunctious and you want to calm him down for mealtime, try that quiet record again. Or if your baby wakes up grumpy or groggy after a nap, play a lively tune and dance around with him. The child may perk right up.

"Eentsy Weentsy Spider"   ages 1 to 3
This song combines singing and finger play, which makes it particularly amusing for young children. You probably remember the tune; if not, make up your own. Here are the words:

The eentsy weentsy spider went up the water spout
Down came the rain and washed the spider out
Out came the sun and dried up all the rain
And the eentsy weentsy spider went up the spout again.
The idea is to accompany each line with an action. Two fingers walking along your child's arm or body can represent the climbing spider; fingers wiggling overhead can be the rain; and expansive movement with the arms can be the sun coming out. Make the actions as flamboyant as you please, because the actions, especially those representing the spider, bring the song to life. They demonstrate that music is not only pleasant to listen to, but it can also be active and fun. Numerous other songs lend themselves to similar games. "This Old Man," for example, can play "nick-nack" on your child's tum, her shoe, her knee, the floor or whatever strikes your fancy.

Keeping Time   ages 1 to 5
Almost as soon as your youngster can sit up and control her movements, she will begin to experiment with rhythms — clapping her hands, stamping her feet, shaking a rattle, beating a pot with a spoon. At first, this is just noisemaking, but gradually she will discover rhythmic patterns she can repeat. At this point, you can encourage her to keep time to a simple song such as "Jingle Bells." Keeping a beat can be tricky and some children cannot do it very well until they are four or five. But as your child learns to follow the beat of a tune, her rhythmic play will become much more satisfying, in addition to helping to prepare her for later music and dance activities. You can also show your youngster how to use her body as a rhythm instrument — pounding her chest, slapping her thighs, clicking her tongue. You might provide a few rhythm toys: a triangle, a tambourine, clappers, bells,

rhythm sticks. Some of these can be made at home, which will enhance their attractiveness in your child's eyes.

Chanting   ages 2 to 4

Children learn to chant before they can really sing. Repetitive chants arise spontaneously from such games as hopscotch and jump rope, and of course, there is that universal chant children use to tease one another: "Nyaa, nyaa, nyaa, nyaa, nyaa, nyaa." However monotonous they may seem, these chants are a useful preliminary to tuneful singing, and you will want to encourage your child to try a few more. "Rain, Rain, Go Away" is similar to the teasing chant. "Pat-a-Cake, Pat-a-Cake" delights young children with its accompanying hand play. "Old MacDonald" is fun for youngsters who cannot yet carry a tune; they chant the parts of the barnyard animals and then join in on the "Ee-yi, ee-yi ooh." While pushing your child on a swing, you might chant, "Swing high, swing low, this is the way Melissa goes." Personalizing the chant adds interest, and if you suit your voice to the height of the swing, you can help convey the idea of changes in pitch. Encourage your child to join in and try to match your variations in pitch.

Moving to the Music   ages 2 to 6

Music invites movement. Even adults find it difficult to sit still to some tunes, and your child is almost certainly a lot less inhibited. From her reaction to the radio and your records, you will know what music moves her most. Play more of it and encourage her to respond. If you can, play it where she can watch herself dance in a full-length mirror. Some pieces suggest interpretive dancing — Khatchaturian's "Saber Dance," for example, and the marches from Bizet's *Carmen* and Verdi's *Aida*. On a different level, there are standard children's songs, such as "The Hokey Pokey" and "Ring Around the Rosie," that call for dancing of a sort. These work best with small groups of children, especially when the children sing as well as dance.

Action Songs   ages 3 to 6

Singing songs that call for actions to accompany them will encourage your child to sing along. A good song of this type, especially if it matches your youngster's mood, is "If You're Happy and You Know It":

    If you're happy and you know it, clap your hands.
    If you're happy and you know it, clap your hands.
    If you're happy and you know it, then your face
        will surely show it.
    If you're happy and you know it, clap your hands.
You can make up a variety of actions that will fit the song's meter.

Have your child stamp her feet, nod her head, wave her arms, touch her nose. "I'm a Little Teapot" calls for more complicated movements and is amusing for older children. And "Here We Go Round the Mulberry Bush" is infinitely adaptable. You and your youngster can sing it as she helps you around the house: "This is the way we make our bed," or "sweep the floor" or "wash our clothes" or "rake the leaves."

Listening Together   ages 3 to 6

You can try this activity as soon as your youngster learns to talk in sentences. Stand, sit or lie down together, listening closely to a piece of music. As you listen, ask your child, "What do you think makes that pretty sound?" or "What do those words make you think of ?" or "What does that sound remind you of ?" Eventually, you can play the game with complex instrumental music. Prokofiev's *Peter and the Wolf* is a good piece to start with because of its helpful narration. With practice, your child will be able to identify the sounds of the orchestral instruments; eventually the youngster may learn to distinguish variations in rhythm, tempo, volume and orchestration, and the effects they have on the emotions the music conveys.

Drawing to Music   ages 3 to 6

If your youngster likes to draw, this is a particularly appealing activity that encourages both attentive listening and creativity. Place a large piece of paper on the floor by the radio or record player, and as your child listens, ask her to draw whatever the music suggests: a feeling, action, character or design. Any music will do, but instrumental pieces give the imagination free rein. *Peter and the Wolf* is a good choice for this activity, too, because the narration mentions but does not fully describe the action that the music is intended to suggest. Tchaikovsky's *Nutcracker* is another children's favorite that is both lively and evocative. Beethoven's *Sixth Symphony*, the "Pastorale," with its hunting horns and thunderstorm, is another possibility.

Making Instruments
ages 3 to 6

You can help your child make her own simple instruments, which will stimulate hours of creative musical activity. An empty adhesive-bandage box with a few dried beans in it makes a fine shaker; a coffee can with a plastic top can be a drum; and a comb covered with wax paper makes a serviceable kazoo. A slightly more elaborate project is to make a tambourine out of two pie tins: Place a handful of dried beans or pebbles in an aluminum pie plate. Cover the plate with a matching plate laid face down. Tape the edges of the pie plates together, or punch holes in the edges and sew the plates together tightly with brightly-colored yarn. Decorate the tambourine with crepe paper or ribbons, and your child has a festive rhythm instrument.

Dramatic Play

"Let's pretend" is an important, even vital, part of every child's development. Dramatic play — the acting out of make-believe roles and situations — teaches a youngster a wealth of things about her world and herself and her emotions. She learns to understand experiences by re-creating them again and again, to get along with people, to make decisions and to solve problems. Pretend play also provides a healthy way to vent fears and frustrations and to experience in a harmless fashion such forbidden desires as driving the family car or cooking over a hot stove. As a parent, you can enhance the benefits of dramatic play by initiating and guiding any number of stimulating activities.

Make-believe does not really become part of a child's play until she nears her second birthday. An 18-month-old may begin by pretending to drink from an empty cup or eat with an empty spoon. You can encourage this play by also pretending to eat and by asking, "Are you eating something? What is it? May I taste it?" Between the ages of two and three, your child may extend her pretend play to dolls and stuffed animals, feeding them, wrapping them in a blanket, putting them to bed — all things that she herself experiences in real life. In the fourth year, her imagination may soar: A simple paper crown can transform her into a beautiful princess living in a fabulous wonderland castle. And by five, your child may be ready to act out a wide variety of complex characters and situations.

A good time for you to encourage dramatic play is after an event that makes an impression on her: a television show, a storytelling session, a visit to the doctor. Yet the day-to-day happenings of a child's life form a continual theme for pretend play; a child works out her everyday concerns by literally playing around with them until she can assimilate them. While you can enrich this make-believe by subtly entering into it, you should be careful not to dominate it. Watch for cues, then follow your child's lead. If she picks up a pretend telephone and speaks into it, for example, pick up your own pretend telephone and start a lively conversation to which your child can respond and expand her verbal skills. Children learn a great deal about pretend play by watching their parents pretend.

Dress-Up Characters ages 2 to 6

When your two-year-old begins to clomp around the house in Mommy's shoes, she is ready for some dress-up make-believe. Now is the time to start saving your old hats, scarves, blouses, belts, shoes, jewelry, gloves, pocketbooks and wigs, all of which can go into what you might call your child's prop-box. Various household odds and ends can also go into the prop-box: pots and pans, wooden spoons, keys, towels, whatever looks like it might spark your youngster's ever-growing imagination. You will find, too, that aluminum foil is indispensable for police officer's badges, magic wands, even a knight's shining armor.

You may wish to suggest a role and help with the costume at first. After a checkup at the doctor's office, for example, your four-year-old might easily be outfitted in an old white shirt and equipped with a meat baster for a syringe, cotton balls and adhesive strip bandages, perhaps even a toy stethoscope. In this kind of make-believe play, she will build understanding and vocabulary by mimicking the doctor; she may also ease her fears of injections and other medical treatments. And your child will love seeing her dress-up character in a full-length mirror.

As they realize what fun it is to play dress-up, children can transform themselves into an endless array of characters: bus driver, traffic officer, bulldozer operator, fire fighter, nurse, queen, movie star — whatever that busy little head conjures up. If you think that your child's interest in dress-up is particularly strong, you may wish to enlist the youngster's help in setting up and maintaining several prop-boxes with specialized items for various roles.

A Weather Game ages 3 to 6

In this bit of dramatic play, you and your child join as a team to act out your responses to various kinds of weather. You might, for example, suggest that it is raining, and so you have to cover your heads with a newspaper or an umbrella. Next, you come to a puddle. What to do? She jumps across, and you do, too. You might expand the game by asking your child to select a particular season of the year and act out a few of its characteristics. If she picks winter, for example, you might ask, "Are you cold?" If she says yes, the two of you can pretend to shiver. You could continue by asking, "Does it snow in winter?" If she says yes, then you can suggest that the two of you make a pretend snowman or toss pretend snowballs. This kind of open-ended play helps your youngster learn how to make believe and also imparts some useful information about the real world.

Acting Out an Experience ages 3 to 6

Dramatizing an experience is one way a child has of absorbing and understanding it. Pretending helps him deal with both pleasant and unpleasant events; he play-acts the occasion over and over again until he has mastered it.

One way to encourage him is by telling a story about a child who has an adventure; it can be a thinly disguised tale of an experience your child has already had, or one he is about to have. As you relate the story, suggest that your youngster act out various parts of the event. If the child is re-creating a recent visit to a zoo, for example, stuffed animals can stand in for the real ones. You can suggest that your child play zookeeper, or he can play himself if he likes, reacting with awe to the lions and giraffes and brightly colored parrots.

If your youngster has gone through a particularly painful or frightening experience, he may wish to play the doer in the story, rather than the victim he may actually feel himself to be. This kind of role reversal will give him a new perspective on the experience, as well as a good challenge in dramatic play.

A Pretend Train Ride   ages 3 to 6

A certain amount of structure is required for this game, and it will be more fun if there are several children to join in. First, you will need a train. A row of chairs or boxes makes a good train. But instead of setting the stage yourself, ask the children what would make a good train and let them help decide on and arrange the props. Most likely, more than one youngster will want to be the conductor or engineer of the train. Explain about some of the other people who work for railroads: the ticket agent in the train station, the switch operator, the baggage handler. And the train will need passengers, of course. Someone could even pretend to be the train's whistle.

A few additional props will make the game of pretend train travel more interesting and enjoyable: shopping bags for luggage, cut-up paper for tickets and money, a bell for the engineer, travel posters for the scenery the passengers see out the windows. After the game has been played awhile, you might suggest that the children exchange roles. This will help the youngsters develop the social skills of cooperation and will also give them the experience of being followers as well as leaders.

Creating a Miniworld   ages 4 to 6
As your preschooler develops greater small-muscle coordination, he will be able to manipulate tiny objects with more skill. Now, dolls, cars and miniature people and animals may become favored playthings — along with miniature castles, houses, garages, farms and zoos for them to live in.

The miniworld is a valuable play experience for your child because it allows him to be in total control of his creation. The youngster can create complex, extended stories and direct a large cast of characters, some of whom he may endow with magical abilities to vault walls and even fly. Girls, of course, often become fascinated with dolls. But all youngsters tend to be interested in pretend dramas of family life, and boys should not be discouraged from playing with dolls.

You can help your child build a dollhouse or some other type of miniworld out of cardboard boxes. A large box with cross-section subdividers is one possibility; others include combinations of grocery boxes, cigar boxes and shoe boxes to construct a series of miniature rooms. Children enjoy these rooms without ceilings because they are easy to reach into. Doors and windows can be cut into these rooms, if your child wants them. Tiny boxes such as matchboxes or jewelry boxes make good building blocks for furniture, and the youngster can decorate with poster paints and scraps of material and wallpaper.

Putting On a Puppet Show   ages 4 to 6
If your youngster is interested in puppet play, she might enjoy dramatizing a story, nursery rhyme or song. She may even find it easier to express her thoughts and feelings through the mouth of a puppet than through her own mouth. You can help her get started by acting out a story with puppets yourself, having the puppet ask your child to join in. Another way to begin is to read a favorite story out loud, and then ask your child to act it out with puppets. Once she gets the hang of it, she may go on to make up original stories. The entertainment can be very lively, indeed; it can even include puppet fights, because make-believe permits a child to express her strongest emotions through a puppet without fear of reprimand or of hurting someone's feelings.

Your child can make a basic puppet stage by placing a sheet over a table, which creates a stage and a hidden backstage area where she can manipulate her puppets. A cardboard box with holes cut in the front and rear, and decorated with curtains, will make the playing area even more like a real theater. ∴

Art and Sculpture

The visual arts fulfill an essential need in children to explore and organize their wide, new world. The acts of drawing, painting and shaping objects with their own two hands teach them important new ways of thinking, of creating and of communicating with images as well as with words. Your role as a parent is to offer your youngster encouragement and a wealth of materials, and basically let her take it from there, the more freewheeling the better.

For very young children, art is mostly in the doing. Their interest at first lies not so much in producing a realistic representation of something, but simply in trying out new things to do. Molding, mixing, cutting and brushing are ends in themselves, exciting to discover and experience over and over again. In the process, children enhance their visual and tactile abilities; their motor skills and eye-hand coordination improve; and their language skills grow as they learn action words, directional words and words for tools.

Your youngster is ready for her introduction to art as soon as she is more interested in manipulating crayons than in throwing or eating them. As she begins to scribble or to pound clay, her focus is on how the activity feels; she may not even look at what she is doing. Her attention span will be very short, perhaps only a few minutes. But as your child gains more control over her movements and her imagination expands, you will find her concentrating for longer and longer periods; by the time she is five or six, she may work steadily for up to an hour, proudly completing images of her world.

You can help your child grow artistically by making sure not to impose your own likes and dislikes. You may, for example, prefer painting to sculpture, but sculpture can be enormously satisfying to youngsters; they find great excitement in the textures and in the sense of dimension and permanence. Whatever she is doing, it is important to assure your child that there is no right or wrong in art. She should be encouraged to draw or sculpt whatever she pleases however she pleases, in order to experience to the fullest the joys of adventure and experimentation. Try not to criticize. Original thinking and self-confidence are enough for now; technique can come later. And do not push her to finish a project. It is finished when she loses interest.

Finger Painting
ages 1 to 6

You can introduce your youngster to finger painting even before he has sufficient hand and finger control to mark with crayons or brushes, and by varying the activity, you can keep the child interested in the activity for years. Fingerpaints are widely available at hobby- or art-supply stores, and any surface that is nonabsorbent and easily cleaned will make a good canvas. Formica, plastic and porcelain tabletops do nicely, and so does the inside of a bathtub; aluminum cookie sheets, shiny shelf paper and shirt cardboards also make good canvases. Before you start, you will probably want to dress your budding artist in old clothes or a smock, and spread newspapers or lay down an old sheet. You can then begin by dampening the work surface with a sponge and spooning on a gob of paint. Show your child how to smear the paint with his hands, and then stand back.

When your youngster is just beginning, encourage him to make large, free arm movements using just one color. Later, he can experiment with mixing primary colors to create new hues. He can also try making handprints and thumbprints. After he has produced a picture, you can show him how to transfer it by placing a sheet of paper on top of the painted surface and then peeling them apart. Finger painting is an activity that develops your child's motor control, introduces him to textures and mixing colors, and helps him understand the relationship between his movements and the marks that appear.

Cutting Capers   ages 3 to 6

Before your youngster goes to school, she will probably want to know how to use scissors, and this ability will open up a whole new field of artwork for her. Purchase some good-quality, blunt-nosed scissors, right- or left-handed — whatever seems most comfortable for her. First, have your child hold the scissors with two hands and, with one quick stroke, cut in half a paper straw or a narrow strip of paper while you are holding it. Let her lop off several pieces until she masters the basic stroke. Next, progress to wider pieces of paper and long, continuous cuts, changing to cutting with one hand in the process. At this point, you can suggest that she might like to make some decorations for one of her drawings by cutting a fringed edge on four strips of paper and gluing the pieces to the edges of the drawing. Much later, she can experiment with cutting out silhouettes of familiar objects or cutting a folded piece of paper to make a symmetrical design.

Learning to use scissors will open the door to a multitude of decorative touches, encourage the responsible use of tools and help develop manual dexterity.

Elementary Printing   ages 2 to 6

The rhythm of printing with stampers appeals strongly to children, and they can take pride in creating things that are useful: wrapping paper, for example, or shelf paper or book covers. You can make a simple stamp pad from a clean kitchen sponge or a thick wad of absorbent paper saturated with tempera, food coloring or watercolor. Let your child choose some stampers: small pieces of sponge, cotton balls, empty sewing spools, the rims from juice cans, corks, cookie cutters, or whatever appeals to her artistic senses — and you deem safe and appropriate. Show her how to press the stamps onto the stamp pad and transfer the image to paper, and then allow her imagination to roam free.

Printing will introduce your child to the concept of repeat design and help increase her awareness of the beautiful patterns that occur in nature.

Patchwork Picture   ages 3 to 6
Putting together a collage will help your youngster develop an understanding of composition and introduce him to the artistic possibilities of different colors, shapes and textures. And the hunt for odds and ends to put in a collage is not only great fun, it will help your child begin to see the infinite possibilities the world has to offer for making art. Have your child collect bits of yarn, string, wooden ice-cream sticks, pebbles, sea shells, egg cartons, buttons, stickers, leaves, and pieces of torn and cut-up paper. Once he has an interesting collection, show him how to glue them on a big piece of cardboard or heavy construction paper. He may want to make a design or simply arrange them at random, and he can add paint or crayon to outline areas or accent details. Aside from its artistic value, this activity will help develop your child's dexterity and eye-hand coordination as he manipulates the objects he wants to put in his collage.

Dough Critters   ages 3 to 6
Children enjoy pounding and squeezing clay from an early age, but they may not be ready to create figures until about their fourth birthday. Then, you can buy nontoxic molding clay or make homemade dough in the kitchen, using a simple recipe based on flour, water and salt *(page 105)*. Either way, your youngster will be fascinated to see how she can create a piece of art out of what seems to be nothing at all.

If your choice is homemade dough, your child may enjoy helping you mix and squeeze the dough. When it reaches the right consistency, roll the dough into a ball, then place it on a cookie sheet covered with heavy-duty aluminum foil. Let your youngster go to it, pounding, rolling, squeezing and pinching the dough to make a snake, a hotdog, a pancake, a hamburger, a doughnut, a plate — whatever her imagination suggests. Until she reaches the age of five, she may not care much about making things to keep, so the dough can be stored in an air-tight container and used again and again. If your child does want to preserve a piece, you can air-dry the critter, let your child paint it with tempera or food coloring, and brush several coats of clear nail polish over it.

In addition to stimulating her tactile senses, this activity will demonstrate a basic lesson about combining materials and help her learn how three-dimensional shapes are formed.

Straw-Blow Painting   ages 4 to 6
Painting with tools other than a brush can help your youngster discover whole new approaches to expression. This project requires only that he be able to blow through a straw. He can start by dribbling pools of watercolor or thinned tempera on a piece of paper, then taking a straw and blowing at the paint. It will run across the paper in a spreading design of rivulets. He can add to the fun by experimenting with different colors and blowing them every which way to make an even more colorful and interesting pattern. By showing your youngster the possibilities of other artistic tools, you expand his experience and encourage him to be bold in exploring ways to express himself. This activity will also show him the different sizes a line can have and what happens to colors when they overlap.

Body Tracing   ages 5 to 6
Children are fascinated by their bodies, and body tracing is a way for them to express their interest with a full-size portrait. You or another child will have to help your youngster by making the basic tracing. Ask him to lie down on a large piece of paper, then trace all around his body with a crayon or a felt-tipped marker. Now he can fill in the details of his face, hands, arms, legs and feet; color his eyes and hair; and add clothes and color them, too. This activity will help your child learn more about colors and increase his body awareness and his understanding of the features common to all people — to say nothing of sparking his imagination and creative expression. ⁂

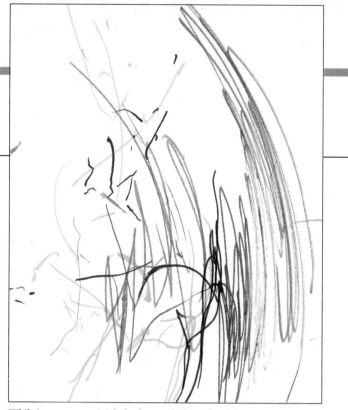

How Children's Art Evolves

It is remarkable how closely children's art parallels their intellectual development. As children move from a self-centered view of the world to one in which they embrace a larger universe, their art follows suit. And because of this parallel growth, very young children draw in much the same way at much the same stage, regardless of cultural differences. Early pictures of people look amazingly similar, whether the young artist is a girl in Texas or a boy in Tibet.

In their efforts to illustrate the world around them, all youngsters progress from scribbling to drawing simple shapes to creating more complex pictures, as shown in these drawings collected by children's art expert Sylvia Feinburg. The stages can overlap considerably; a four-year-old may be deeply engrossed in drawing a house one day and joyously scribbling away the next. Children of equal intelligence often reach the various stages at different ages, of course, as they advance according to their own personal timetables.

Your youngster may begin to scribble at the age of 14 months or so, delighting in the sheer physical activity of moving the crayon around and the bright marks it leaves. As her coordination improves, the whorls and zigzags become more controlled, hinting at wonders to come.

Around the time the child turns three, the scribbles magically turn into shapes — circles, squares, triangles and crosses. A few shapes may suggest boats and houses, yet your youngster is more likely to regard them simply as interesting designs. One day soon, however, she will discover that a circle, or a ball of clay, can be made to symbolize something — a head, perhaps, one that looks to her like her mommy or daddy. With this tremendous leap in thinking, children arrive at the representational stage of artistic development.

In their first pictures and sculptures, children work entirely from their own vantage point, creating things they feel or imagine rather than what they actually see. Accurate color and size are blithely ignored; parts may be missing. It is not until the age of five or six that children's art starts to reflect a determined realism. And then, as the subjective attitudes of early childhood give way to a greater objectivity, your child will become eager to capture life in all its rich detail.

While it may seem trivial, the free scribbling of a two-year-old goes well beyond simple motor activity and, in fact, sets the stage for all writing and drawing. By exploring dots, short and long strokes, and curved lines, children begin to learn the implications of the marker and the limits of the paper and to sense the pleasure of creating a lasting image.

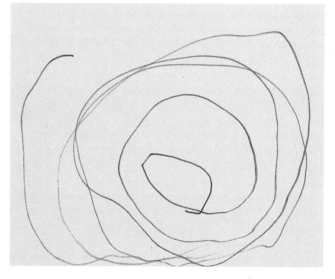

The first recognizable shape a youngster draws is a circle, enchanting in its roundness. This one, which starts as a spiral, reflects sophisticated eye-hand coordination. By saying "I'm making an eggie," the artist showed she had reached another milestone — making the connection between a shape and what it can represent, which is the beginning of art.

Although it contains no specific object, this drawing by a four-year-old is not scribbling. It shows much control and concentration, as well as a capacity to draw an elaborate pattern and to differentiate between figure and background. Long after they learn to create "real" pictures, children still delight in abstract designs; for them, symbols and forms are equally important.

Typical for a three-year-old, this "egg head" drawing combines the child's love of making circles with early efforts to depict a face. Children at this age do not always differentiate between the head and the body; they simply employ familiar shapes in their first people pictures.

A four-year-old's drawings are more recognizable, although often out of proportion. Long, skinny tadpole figures are seen — as are heads with sprouting arms or legs, or hands with missing fingers. The omissions are not significant; the child puts in what matters to him at the moment, and his views of a subject can vary widely from day to day.

When a child is between four and five, letters come into the picture, often combined with scribbles and sketches of people and things. Impulsiveness is the order of the day; objects dance in space, color is indiscriminate and size is still of little consequence.

Found in primitive art throughout history, the sun remains a favorite design of young children today. With its radiating lines, it can easily symbolize an animal, a flower or a face. A picture of the sun is often a child's first step in drawing a human figure.

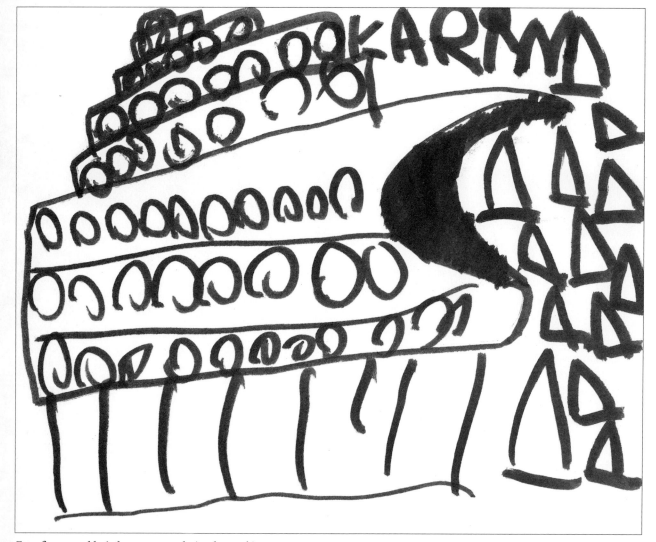

For a five-year-old, circles, squares and triangles combine to portray a steamer bearing down on a flotilla of sailboats and, at upper right, the artist's name. Reality remains elusive at this stage; though Karim probably started out to draw a boat and would identify it as such, he is still clearly enthralled by shapes for their own sake.

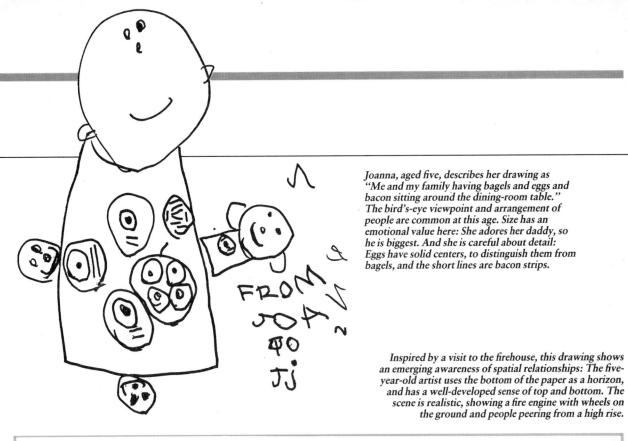

Joanna, aged five, describes her drawing as
"Me and my family having bagels and eggs and
bacon sitting around the dining-room table."
The bird's-eye viewpoint and arrangement of
people are common at this age. Size has an
emotional value here: She adores her daddy, so
he is biggest. And she is careful about detail:
Eggs have solid centers, to distinguish them from
bagels, and the short lines are bacon strips.

Inspired by a visit to the firehouse, this drawing shows
an emerging awareness of spatial relationships: The five-
year-old artist uses the bottom of the paper as a horizon,
and has a well-developed sense of top and bottom. The
scene is realistic, showing a fire engine with wheels on
the ground and people peering from a high rise.

Mathematics

Your child is surrounded by a world of mathematics. Long before he begins to deal with abstract symbols and formulas, he will find math in the things he sees and touches; he will make his first discoveries about space by crawling under chairs and tables, experience his first contact with shape by rolling balls and holding bottles. And as your youngster continues, with your help, to explore the world surrounding him, he will delight in learning how to apply such basic mathematical concepts as classifying, comparing, ordering and counting.

As an infant, your child will happily examine everything within reach. By the time he is two, he may start to classify objects, perhaps by color, or by shape or function — or sometimes by some private logic only he can understand. At about this time, when the child begins to talk, his awareness of such concepts as "big" and "small" develops into the idea of "bigger" and "smaller" as he starts to compare one object with another. At three, your youngster may be ready for the fun of ordering — arranging objects from smallest to largest, from first to next to last. Now his grasp

of math may include the notion of weighing and measuring. At this point, he may begin counting, and by the time the youngster's fifth birthday comes around, he may understand the numbers zero through five and be able to recite the numbers one through 10.

Your role in this wonderful game of learning is to offer your child a wealth of opportunities in his daily activities. Encourage him to explore and experiment, ask questions and draw conclusions. Provide him with things to count, compare and classify — making sure, of course, that they are safe objects too large to swallow. Suggest new words, play games and teach him songs and rhymes that promote math activities. Have him share your daily math experiences: checking prices, weights and sizes when you go shopping; selecting and measuring food in the kitchen; setting the dinner table and sorting the laundry.

Experiences such as these will help your youngster comprehend the role of mathematics in everyday life and will prepare him for formal math training in a way that is stimulating and challenging.

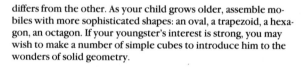

differs from the other. As your child grows older, assemble mobiles with more sophisticated shapes: an oval, a trapezoid, a hexagon, an octagon. If your youngster's interest is strong, you may wish to make a number of simple cubes to introduce him to the wonders of solid geometry.

Putting Away the Silverware   ages 2 to 4
Your youngster will learn about classification — and in the process, acquire a skill useful in helping you with the housework — if you scatter some identical spoons and forks on the table and ask her to sort them. Then you may ask her to return the pieces of silverware to the places where they are kept. As your child progresses, you can make the game more meaningful for her by emptying the contents of the dishwasher utensil compartment on the table and asking the youngster to put away all the various sizes of forks and spoons.

Songs and Rhymes with Numbers   ages 2 to 6
Songs and rhymes are an easy and pleasurable way for children to learn about numbers. Songs with numbers, such as "This Old Man," and rhymes, such as "One, Two, Buckle My Shoe," will teach your youngster to recognize numbers by name long before she understands their meaning. Counting with her fingers as she sings or recites will let her see as well as hear the numbers as she practices using them.

Measuring in Feet   ages 3 to 4
Using standard units to measure distance is a fundamental principle of math — and one that will be more fun for your youngster if the measuring unit is one of his own feet. First help your child trace his foot on a piece of paper and cut out the pattern with

A Shape Mobile   birth to 3 years
Hanging free and gently moving with the air currents, a shape mobile will delight your youngster and serve to familiarize him with geometric forms. To start, cut out a triangle, circle and square from construction paper or cardboard; punch a hole at the top of each item and hang them with lengths of string from the ceiling of the child's room. Let your child examine the mobile; tell him what each shape is and invite him to see how one

scissors. Then make about a dozen paper copies of the pattern. Now ask your child a simple measuring question, such as, "How many of your feet is it from the toy box to the table?" Show him how to line up the paper feet end to end and count them to measure the distance between the two objects. After he has mastered the basics of measuring, you can help him record various distances and compare them in terms of more or less feet. At some point, you may wish to explain the difference in size between his foot and the 12-inch foot used in standard measurement.

Storybook Counting   age 3
Children are generally glad to be growing up, and at the age of three, they are especially interested in stories built around the number three — "Three Little Pigs," "Three Blind Mice" and "Goldilocks and the Three Bears," for example. These old favorites reinforce your child's concept of "threeness," particularly when you emphasize the number three each time it appears in the story. You might also find it enjoyable to go on explorations around the house looking for objects in groups of three.

Recognizing Patterns   ages 3 to 5
You can help your child gain a basic math skill by introducing her to patterns. Using large colored buttons or blocks, create simple patterns by alternating the colors, such as AABB or ABAB. At first, ask your youngster to duplicate the pattern. Later, you may wish to have the child fill in spaces you have left open in the pattern, or you may ask her to develop her own pattern and tell you about it. As your child gains insight into patterns, you can go on an expedition with her to discover patterns that occur all over the house or yard.

Lighter and Heavier   ages 3 to 5
Learning about weight can begin with objects of almost identical size but different weights — a table-tennis ball and a golf ball, for instance, or one lunch bag filled with sand and another with leaves. Ask your youngster to lift these objects and describe them as light or heavy depending on how easy or how hard they are to lift. Next, you may wish to move on to objects of less obviously contrasting weight and objects of varying sizes and shapes. By comparing an object that is large but light with one that is small but heavy — an empty detergent box compared to a hammer, for instance — your child will learn that weight cannot always be determined by size or appearance.

Who's Taller?   ages 3 to 5
Your youngster's natural fascination with his growing body will make this math game particularly fun. To begin, take two dolls of different heights and stand them side by side on the table. Ask your child which one is taller. Then, put the two dolls on different levels and ask him to point out which is the taller one now. Discuss his answer with him, and then ask what he needs to do to determine which doll is really the taller of the two. He will learn

that measuring by perception requires a common base line — in this case, a common surface for the dolls to stand on.

Smaller and Bigger   ages 3 to 5
Comparison is more interesting than simple classification because your child learns to judge an object not simply by its own appearance but in relation to other objects as well. Collect a number of items that are more or less identical in appearance but of different sizes — for example, bath-size and personal-size bars of soap; a tablespoon and a teaspoon; a dinner plate and a butter plate; regular and travel-size tubes of toothpaste. Then mix the objects up and spread them out on a table or the floor. Hold up one item and ask your youngster if she can find another one like it. Ask her to tell you which one is smaller and which one is larger. Learning about relative size will help develop her sense of logic as well as math skills.

Balancing Scale   ages 3 to 6
Once your youngster feels comfortable with the concept of weight, she can use her newfound knowledge to compare objects on a balancing scale. An easy way to improvise a balancing scale is to tie with string a paper cup to each end of a coat hanger. Hold the scale lightly with your thumb, allowing it to swing freely by the hook. First, your child can observe what happens when two objects of equal weight are placed in the cups. Then, she can see what happens when two objects of obviously different weight go into the scales. Continue the exercise by asking her to predict what will happen when various other objects are placed in the cups. You may wish to ask her why she thinks one object will be heavier than another, and then discuss with her the results of the experiment. She will enjoy testing herself and the experiment will expand her understanding of weight from "light" and "heavy" to "lighter" and "heavier."

Learning about Zero   ages 3 to 5

As your child advances from the numbers one, two and three to learn four, you will want to teach him also about that mysterious number on the other side: zero. Help him make four cutouts of animals or other interesting objects and pin them on the bulletin board one at a time; encourage your youngster each time to count how many figures there are on the board. Then, remove the figures one at a time, while he counts in reverse. When they are all gone, explain to your child that there are now zero figures on the board, that zero is what we use to indicate that there are no more left. If he is learning to write, you can show him what zero looks like and how empty the shape of it appears compared to the other numbers he knows.

Putting Blocks in Order   ages 3 to 5

You can expand your youngster's ability to compare by introducing another important skill — placing things in order. Take five progressively larger blocks and arrange them in a line, smallest to largest. Then, give your child another five blocks and ask her if she would like to build a line of blocks just like the one she sees before her. You may wish to vary the game by removing the second and fourth blocks and asking her to fill in missing spaces from her pile of blocks. Or you can let her sort the blocks however she wants and ask her to tell you about her arrangement. As she learns to put things in order, she will progress from sets to series, arranging objects from a given point in a given direction.

Setting the Table   ages 2 to 6

This ongoing activity involves comparing and counting; it starts off quite simply when your child is two or three and advances in complexity as his skill increases. To begin with, ask him to set a low table with four places, using at first only placemats, paper plates and cups. He will want to get the correct number of items at each place, and he may find it easier and more amusing if he counts out loud as he selects items and places them on the table. It does not matter if he arranges them helter-skelter at each place; proper order can come later. Gradually add napkins and plastic utensils. As his abilities grow, real flatware, glasses and dinnerware will pose a new challenge and offer a new sense of accomplishment. By the time he is five or so, he may even be able to set the family table for lunch or dinner — and feel very proud, both of his math skills and of the way he is helping you.

Fun with a Calculator   ages 3 to 5

Children love to play with things that belong to their parents. Giving your youngster a chance to play with an inexpensive, hand-held calculator will help familiarize him with numbers, including the number zero. Show him how to fill the screen of the calculator with numbers, then show him how to erase them. You may wish to join in the play by calling out numbers and helping him push the correct button to make it appear on the screen. As he learns to manipulate the buttons, you may offer some basic calculations for him to perform. Tell your youngster that two plus two equals four; when he pushes the right buttons, the results will seem like magic.

A Scrapbook of Numbers   ages 3 to 5

Even though your preschooler may casually recite numbers from one to 10, the idea that a number represents a certain value can be difficult for her to understand at first. Placing an appropriate number of objects next to a numeral in a homemade scrapbook will help her to grasp the concept of numbers as quantitative symbols. To begin, sit down with your child and help her prepare a scrapbook from construction paper or shirt cardboards. In bold printing, clearly number the pages from one to five or so. Then browse through old magazines looking for pictures of one chair, two mountains, three people or whatever suits her fancy. Let her cut out the pictures and paste them onto the scrapbook pages, and encourage her to add pages with higher numbers and more objects as she begins to grasp the idea.

Lily Pond   ages 4 to 6

You can enhance your child's command of the numbers zero through four with a game that involves counting items and sets, as well as doing basic addition and subtraction. Make a lily pond on the floor with four saucers for lily pads and four pieces of green construction paper for frogs. To start, ask your child to do simple counting with the frogs alone, including zero frogs when they have all left their pads to swim in the pond. Then, you can progress to sets by having the frogs share the pads in different combinations; for example, two sets of two frogs on a pad, or one set of three frogs on a pad with one frog left over on a different pad. You can introduce her to addition by having frogs jump out of the water onto a pad. You can ask, for example, "If we have one frog on a pad and one more jumps on, how many frogs are on the pad now?" And you can illustrate subtraction by removing one of the lily pads and asking, "If one of the pads sinks to the bottom, how many are left?"

Card Games   ages 4 to 6
Playing with a deck of cards is an enjoyable way for children to practice the skills of classifying, comparing, sorting and counting. Smaller children can become familiar with numbers and shapes by unstructured play with cards. And older youngsters can learn valuable math skills from such games as High Card, Old Maid and Go Fish.

High Card, for example, is a game for two players that involves counting and simple comparison. Remove the face cards from the deck and deal the remaining 40 cards to the players. The players turn over the top cards on their stacks, and the player

with the higher card takes both cards and places them in a winnings pile. If the players turn up cards of identical value, they then play a tie-breaker hand in which each deals three more cards face down and a fourth face up. The player whose face-up card is higher wins all the cards played in the tie-breaker hand and adds them to his winnings pile. If there is yet another tie, the tie-breaker sequence is repeated until one player wins all of the accumulated cards. Regular play then resumes. When the playing stacks are depleted, the players turn to their winnings piles and continue playing with them until one youngster has won the entire deck of cards.

Adding and Subtracting Necklace   ages 5 to 6
This activity is an engaging way for your child to learn basic addition and subtraction. Make a necklace out of string and large beads or plastic curtain rings. Have her throw dice and decide whether she wants to add on or take off the number of pieces indicated by the dice. Encourage your youngster to use such terms as "more," "less," "plus" and "minus" to introduce her to the basic vocabulary of math.

Sets and Singles   ages 5 to 6
At the age of five, a child may have real command of the numbers zero through five only. However, he can handle many more items with his limited knowledge by using sets and singles. For example, if the youngster has nine toy soldiers, he can count out sets of two soldiers four times, with one single; or three sets of

three soldiers and zero singles; or two sets of four soldiers with one single. With the knowledge of five, your child can actually handle as many as 29 items — five sets of five with four singles. By means of this mathematical activity, your youngster will gain an elementary acquaintance of numerical bases, which will be valuable later on in school when he starts learning about multiplication and division.

Where Does It Belong?   ages 5 to 6
A satisfying step for your child in math development comes when he finds that something may belong in more than one group at the same time. To help him make this discovery, gather together a variety of toys and household items: a car, an airplane, a wagon, a bird, an apple, a ball of yarn, an orange, a Teddy bear, a doll — items that can be grouped in several ways, depending on what characteristic is chosen. Spread out the objects and ask your youngster first to sort them by large groupings — toys and food, for example. Next you may narrow the groupings — things that fly and things that walk. Then you may wish to try multiple groupings — things that are red and have wheels and things that are yellow and soft.

Once your child gets the hang of multiple groupings, he may enjoy the challenge of this game: Make two circles of string on the floor, side by side but not overlapping. Then, take several similarly shaped objects, such as blocks, none of which are blue, and a group of blue objects, none of which are blocks. Mix them together and scatter them on the floor. Ask your child to classify the blocks in one circle and the blue objects in the other circle. Then offer him a blue block and ask your youngster to place it where it belongs. If he places it in one circle, ask him why he did not put it in the other circle and discuss his reasoning. He may position the block between the two circles. Or the child may change the shapes of the circles so that they overlap, to suggest that the blue block, having attributes of both groups, belongs in both circles. However the youngster decides, the game will encourage a flexible approach and independent thinking in seeking solutions to problems.

Science

Science, in its broadest sense, is the study of all nature, and as a parent, you do not have to be a scientist to help your child enjoy the wonders of the world around him. Your main role in developing your youngster's scientific potential is to provide the encouragement and materials he needs to explore his environment.

Any child is ready to begin simple science activities if he is curious about his surroundings, asks questions and shows an interest in collecting objects and organizing them into some kind of a pattern. Because young children learn best by doing, actual hands-on experiences and experiments are the most meaningful to them.

A youngster's comprehension of basic scientific concepts will, of course, vary with age. A two-year-old may notice that one toy floats while another sinks. From this simple beginning, the child will progress in a year or so to the fun of experimenting on his own with other toys and discovering differences in weight, texture and other characteristics. He will decide for himself which toys are easier to manipulate than others: which feel softer, harder or rougher; which

sound more pleasurable when banged; which have little or no sound at all. A year later, he may be able to understand simple explanations for such diverse physical properties.

Be on the lookout for signs of scientific curiosity in your child's play, and casually follow up with questions and comments appropriate to his age and level of understanding. When your son brings back an insect and wants to keep it and care for it, for example, you might start by asking, "What do you think it needs to eat?" Most likely, he will have some ideas on the subject, followed by more questions for you about how to make a home for his new friend.

At this early stage, the goal is not to teach hard facts, abstract concepts or scientific terminology. Rather, your child should find delight in beginning to learn how his world works. In the process, he will start to absorb the basic processes that underlie all scientific inquiry: questioning and comparing, making sensitive observations, describing and identifying, searching for cause and effect, trying experiments and testing conclusions by making reasoned predictions about how his experiments will turn out.

Exploring with a Magnifying Glass   ages 3 to 6
With the aid of an inexpensive magnifying glass, you can encourage your child to take greater notice of the world around her and help sharpen her powers of observation. Go on a magnifying-glass expedition with her, either inside or outside the house. Have her pick out objects to study under the glass — a feather, a piece of bread, an orange peel, a worm, a leaf, a toothbrush. The possibilities are endless. Ask her what looks different about each object when it is under the glass. What can she see that she did not notice before? If you live in an area where snow falls in winter, you can try this special variation of the activity: Have your child catch snowflakes as they fall and examine their differences under the magnifying glass. Begin by making a platform for the snowflakes, so they can be easily seen: Cover a piece of cardboard with dark-colored felt and place the board in the freezer for about 20 minutes so that the snowflakes will not melt on contact. Then go outside and collect a batch of snowflakes on the felt. As your child studies them under the glass, point out that each snowflake has a uniquely beautiful pattern, and ask her to describe the shapes she sees. Explain that a snowflake is formed by water vapor in the clouds that freezes into crystals, and that these crystals then join together to form snowflakes.

Finding Out about Air   ages 3 to 4
The concept of "air" as something other than empty space is difficult for young children to grasp. Point out to your child that although we cannot see air, we can see and feel its effects. Invite your child to close his eyes and listen to the wind as it rustles the leaves of a tree. Toss some blades of grass into the air and watch them blow away.

To help your child understand that air, although invisible, has a mass, try this simple kitchen demonstration: Stuff a dry paper towel into an empty drinking glass; next, fill a large, tall transparent container with water and gently hold the drinking glass upside down in the container.

Explain to your youngster that the water is not entering the glass because the glass is already full of air. To emphasize the point, lift the glass out of the water and show your child the still-dry towel. Now let the child return the glass to the water. Encourage him to tilt it slightly and watch the air from the glass escape in bubbles. Explain to the youngster that bubbles are made by air trapped in water.

Making a Rainbow   ages 2 to 3
Young children have a fascination with rainbows. You can help your child understand how rainbows occur in nature by making a rainbow of your own on a wall of your home.

Put a small mirror in a clear glass container; tilt the mirror slightly by placing a small, thin object beneath one end of it. Then place the container on a sunny window sill. Show your youngster how the mirror reflects sunlight onto one of the walls in the room. Next, let the child pour water into the container until the mirror is half covered. The spot of light on the wall should now be transformed into one consisting of many colors. Explain to your child that this little rainbow, or color spectrum, was made by the water's separating the sunlight into its colored parts. You can continue by saying to your youngster that a real rainbow comes about in much the same fashion, but with raindrops instead of a dish of water separating the colors of sunlight.

Learning Cause and Effect — ages 3 to 4

Using everyday events and objects, you can help your child begin to learn from an early age the relationship between cause and effect in the physical world. You should encourage her to think about causes after a puzzling event. For example, when the paste dries in an open jar, help your youngster figure out what might have caused the paste to dry. Was it that the liquid in the paste evaporated into the air?

Besides looking back and discovering what caused an object to change, you can encourage your child to look ahead and predict what effect a particular action will have on a particular object. Pop a balloon with a pin. Stir chocolate into milk. Sharpen a pencil. Drop an apple into a bowlful of water. Just before each action, you should ask your child, "What do you think will happen?" Then observe with the youngster whether her prediction was correct. The ability to think ahead about changes is an early step in reasoning.

Observing Insects — ages 3 to 4

If children are encouraged at an early age to examine insects, they may never develop fear or loathing for these interesting creatures. Instead, a familiarity with insects can help youngsters develop a sense of wonder and compassion for all living things. Search with your child for the homes of insects — under a rock or a piece of bark, in a pile of leaves or a chunk of soil. Notice with your child what each animal does — what it eats, how it flies or moves. You should encourage your youngster to watch each small animal at work, whether it is an ant carrying a bit of leaf or a spider spinning a web.

Your child also can learn how to attract insects to a particular spot for study. On a summer day, make a small amount of sugar water; using an eyedropper or a spoon, have the youngster place a few drops of the mixture on an outdoor window sill. During the next day or so, you should observe with your child any insects that may come to the sugar water. As another experiment, you may wish to put out a little salt-water solution. Your child will see that the salt water does not attract insects; you can explain to the youngster that sugar is special because it is a food energy source, while salt is not.

Investigating Dirt — ages 3 to 5

Backyard dirt is full of interesting things for you and your child to look at and touch. Dig a quart or so of dirt and spread it out on an outdoor table covered with newspaper. Let your child search through the dirt for insects, plants, rocks and other objects. You may wish to have the youngster use a magnifying glass or a sifter to help in the search.

Explain to your child that dirt is composed of small pieces of rock and decayed plants and animals. If possible, you might find it interesting to examine clay and sandy soils as well as more loamy soil and talk about the differences among them. Discuss how some plants have trouble growing in sandy soil because it does not contain enough decayed plants and animals — the nutrients that plants need to grow strong and healthy. Clay soil can present problems, as well, but for a different reason: Heavy clay soil does not drain water very effectively, and plants in it tend to become waterlogged.

Insulating Ice Cubes — ages 3 to 5

Your child can learn about insulation by wrapping ice cubes in a variety of materials and seeing which cubes melt first. Get together some bubble wrap, some aluminum foil, a cotton dishcloth, some tissue paper and some clear plastic wrap. Let your youngster help tie the materials around the ice cubes, then place the wrapped cubes on a tray. Have her return to the tray from time to time to check the progress of the experiment. Discuss with the child why insulators are necessary and why some insulators are better than others. Have her think of the things she uses for her own insulation, such as her hat, coat and mittens, and the blanket on her bed.

Tracing Shadows — ages 2 to 4

Your child's discovery of her shadow can lead to some basic lessons about the sun and its perceived movement during the day. Choose a sunny spot on a sidewalk or a driveway; ask your child to stand on the spot and then trace around her shadow with chalk. Several hours later, return with her to the spot. Trace your youngster's shadow again with chalk. She will see that the two tracings of her shadow are in different locations. Explain to the child that because the earth turns slowly, the sun's position in the sky changes, and the length and position of shadows also change. You should encourage your child to notice changes in other shadows during the day, such as those formed by trees, houses and fences.

Building Bridges
ages 3 to 4

By building a simple paper bridge with your child, you can show him how adjusting the design of a structure can make it stronger. For this activity, you will need two books of about equal thickness, a handful of pennies and a four-by-eight-inch strip of typing or construction paper. Begin by positioning the books four inches apart on a table or on the floor. Pretend that the space between the books is a river. Now place the paper across the river to create a bridge. Ask your child how many pennies — or cars — he thinks can park safely on the bridge. Have him attempt to park one car on the bridge. The structure will bend; it is too weak. Now let your youngster fold up the sides of the paper to make a new, stronger bridge. See how many pennies this new structure will hold. Explain to your youngster that some real bridges have sides similar in design to his paper bridge; remind him to look for such bridges on your next car trip.

Magnetic Attraction   ages 4 to 5

Your child may already have discovered what fun it is to play with the little magnets used to stick notes on the refrigerator door. Further exploration — now with a bigger, stronger magnet — can be used to show him how objects are made of different materials and how these differences are not always obvious to the eye. First, explain that magnets are special because they are attracted to other iron objects — and only to those objects. Demonstrate this to your child by having him test several iron objects, as well as other metal and nonmetal objects, with the magnet. Now explore your house or yard with your child. Have him select objects to test, and ask him to think beforehand whether or not the magnet will stick to the objects. Through these simple experiments, your youngster will learn about predicting and testing, two fundamental scientific processes.

Water and Weather   ages 3 to 6

By means of a few simple kitchen activities you can show your child how water takes different forms. With her help, fill an ice-cube tray with water, then place it in the freezer. An hour or so later, remove the tray and discuss with her how the cold air in the freezer has transformed the water into ice. Let her handle the ice cubes to feel how cold they are.

Next, put the cubes into a saucepan, preferably one made of clear, heatproof glass. With your child watching from a safe distance, heat the cubes on the stove until they melt. She will see the ice turn back into water. Then draw a line with crayon outside the pan — or inside, if you are using a metal pan — to indicate the water level. Boil the water until enough has evaporated to show a marked drop in the water level. Ask your child where she thinks the water has gone; explain that it has turned into vapor and become part of the air. Finally, place a cool, dry lid over the pan until the lid's underside is covered with drops of water. Explain that the vapor has condensed onto the cool lid and has turned into water again.

These water activities offer an excellent opportunity to introduce your child to basic weather concepts. Describe for your youngster how the sun heats water on earth until it evaporates into the air, just as it did in the saucepan. Eventually, the evaporated water condenses to form droplets of water in clouds, just as the droplets formed on the saucepan lid. Explain to your child that when the clouds get too heavy with condensed water, the water falls back to earth as rain.

Growing Plants from Seeds   ages 3 to 4

Watching a seed grow into a plant teaches a child how living things must be nurtured to thrive. Choose large seeds that sprout easily and grow quickly, such as beans or grapefruit seeds. Plant three or four seeds in a styrofoam cup filled with potting soil. Put several additional seeds on a wet paper towel in a glass jar. Place both containers on a sunny window sill; keep the soil and paper towel damp but not soaked. Your child will be able to see the seeds on the towel germinate; tell her that the seeds under the soil are experiencing the same changes. Now put the seeds from the towel in with the seeds in the cup and tell her that most plants need soil as well as water and light to flourish. If possible, you should transplant the seedlings to an outdoor garden after two weeks. Your youngster can take responsibility for the plants by watering and weeding them.

Collecting and Classifying   ages 3 to 6

Young children love to collect outdoor objects, such as stones, feathers, shells and berries. These collections present a fine opportunity for learning how to compare, sort and classify. Encourage your child to put together a collection by accompanying her on an exploration walk. You should take along a paper or plastic bag in which to carry the collected items. Once home, have your child spread out her acquisitions on the floor or on a table. Ask her how the items are similar and how they are different. Then have the youngster suggest a way of sorting the items; leaves, for example, might be sorted by shape, rocks by size and flowers by color. You may wish to provide small containers to help the child separate the sorted items.

Once the sorting has been completed, you may wish to ask your child to sort the items again, this time using different criteria. Flowers, for example, could be sorted according to the number of petals, rocks by color, leaves by size. On a cold or rainy day, the two of you can enjoy this activity by collecting objects around the house, such as buttons and pieces of fabric. You may wish to offer suggestions, but always let your youngster decide for herself how the objects are to be classified; this will encourage her to use her own reasoning skills.

Making a Friction Car
ages 3 to 4
A simple lesson about friction and how to overcome it can be demonstrated with an empty box of tissues and two plastic straws. Place the box on a table and ask your youngster if he can blow the box across the table. Help him understand that the box does not move because it is rubbing against the table; friction is holding it back. Now put the straws under the box and ask your child to try again; the box should move easily. Explain that the straws, because they keep the box from touching the table and because they roll like wheels, allow the box to move. Discover with your youngster other objects around the house and yard that use the same principle, such as a vacuum cleaner, a wheelbarrow, a table on wheels, even the family car. Prompt him to imagine how much more difficult it would be to move these heavy objects if they were not on wheels.

Penny Chemistry   ages 3 to 4
The idea that one substance reacts with another to change its characteristics is the basis of chemistry. For an experiment that will help your child understand a little chemistry, put ¼ cup of vinegar and a teaspoon of salt into a glass and have your child drop three or four tarnished pennies into the solution. Leave the pennies overnight; in the morning, they will be shiny clean. Explain to your child that the copper in pennies reacts to chemicals in the air, which turns the pennies dark; they become shiny when the copper reacts to the salt-and-vinegar solution.

The Skin on Water   ages 3 to 4
Children may wonder how some insects, such as water striders, are able to walk on water. Using a glass and some pennies — or other coins — you can show your youngster that the surface of water is stronger than it seems. To begin the experiment, fill the glass to the rim with water, and ask your child what he thinks will happen if some coins are dropped into the glass. After he has made his prediction, let him drop coins into the glass one at a time; urge him to place them carefully so that they do not splash. As he adds coins he will see that the water can actually rise above the rim of the glass. Explain that the water in the glass has a kind of invisible skin called surface tension that is strong enough to hold it together and keep it from overflowing — but only for a

while. Your young researcher might also have fun making a guess at how many coins can be dropped in before the surface skin finally breaks and sends water running over the rim of the glass. In addition to demonstrating one of the fascinating properties of water, this activity embodies the basic scientific methods of predicting what will happen and testing a hypothesis.

Starlight, Star Bright   ages 4 to 5
You can introduce your child to the basics of astronomy by explaining that the sun is one of the many stars that fill the sky, but since those other stars are so far away, they appear to us as small twinklings. Also explain to your youngster that stars are in the sky all the time, even if we can see them only at night, when the sun is not filling the sky with its bright light. To illustrate this, have your child take a flashlight outside during the day and shine the light around; point out how dim the light is. Look up at the sky and note that there are no stars to be seen. After dark, on a cloudless night, go back outside together with the flashlight and observe how bright it looks when you turn it on. And gaze up at the sky to see the twinkling stars.

Making Sound Waves   ages 4 to 6
Using ordinary objects, you can demonstrate to your youngster how sound travels through the air: Stretch a rubber band and pluck it; hold a ruler against the edge of a table and twang it; hang a saucepan lid from a string and strike it with a spoon. Let your child see, hear and feel these objects vibrate. Then, explain that the vibrations from these objects make the air around them shake; when the shaking air reaches her ear, her eardrum also shakes, and she hears the sound.

With a small homemade telephone, you can show your child how sound travels through objects as well as through the air. For this activity, you will need a 20-foot-long piece of thin string and two empty juice cans. Poke a hole in the end of each can; working from the outside to the inside, pull the string ends through the holes and knot the ends on the inside of each can. Hold one can and let your child hold the other as you walk in opposite directions until the string is pulled taut. Have your child hold her can to her ear while you whisper into your can, then reverse roles and let her whisper into her can. Explain to your child that her voice is making the string vibrate and that the string is carrying those vibrations from her can to yours.

Transforming Food   ages 4 to 6
Using your kitchen as a science center, you can help your youngster understand how things other than water can be transformed into different forms, shapes and textures. Food, in particular, can be used to demonstrate how things undergo change. Let your child observe while you cook — and help you, if he wishes. Have him mash potatoes; show him how you cut potatoes into rounds for frying them. Let him feel the brittle pieces of pasta before you put them into a pot of boiling water to soften and cook. Show him how dried rice swells up and doubles in amount when cooked. Eggs can be especially interesting to your child: Have him crack an egg into a bowl and let him touch it. Ask him to describe how the egg feels: wet? sticky? runny? Next, boil two other eggs in a saucepan. Take one of these eggs out of the water after three minutes, run it under cold water, then crack it open. Ask your child to describe how this egg differs in appearance from the first one. Explain that the hot water has changed the inside of the egg. Finally, after the third egg has cooked for 10 minutes, remove it from the saucepan. Run it under cold water, have your child peel off the egg's hard shell, and ask him "Now what has changed about the inside of the egg?" ❖

Computers: Partners in Learning

Computers have become an everyday part of our lives and of the lives of our children. Youngsters encounter computers in schools and libraries, in stores and offices, and more and more frequently, children have access to computers in their homes.

If you own a computer, you are undoubtedly aware of its usefulness in managing your business or running your household. The computer also can be a first-rate learning tool for your child. It is an infinitely patient and practically indestructible teacher and playmate. And it can be equipped with a variety of simple software programs to provide your child with games and activities that are both stimulating and fun.

Experts in education are studying the value of teaching early-learning concepts on the computer rather than through more traditional methods. While no firm conclusions have been reached about the value of learning from a computer, the prevailing wisdom seems to be that there is no need to purchase a computer for the sole purpose of teaching your child. But if you already happen to own a computer, it can help your youngster begin learning important skills that will be useful in his preschool years and once he goes to school.

A Wealth of Benefits

You may wonder what specific benefits a toddler or preschooler can derive from such a sophisticated piece of machinery as a computer. In fact, the learning effects are broad and far-reaching: Research shows that children generally gain self-confidence and feel a sense of authority when they are controlling the machine, whether they are typing one letter of the alphabet over and over, or are engaged in a learning game.

In addition, computer play can do much to promote creativity in children; after viewing the results of his play on the computer screen, your youngster may become more eager to produce new images, words or sounds. Fine motor skills also are enhanced by working on a computer: As his fingers enter information into the computer and your child tracks the results of his entries on the computer screen, both his eye movement and his eye-hand coordination are stimulated.

But perhaps the most important benefit of all derived from computer play is the development of intellect, of your youngster's ability to think and to learn. Computer play kindles logic and memory, develops a child's problem-solving ability and introduces the concept of cause and effect. Some software programs ask your youngster to make choices at various stages that lead the program to another level of play or to a particular conclusion. The youngster soon comes to learn that each decision he makes affects the program's outcome.

From Toddlerhood On

Most experts agree that a child is ready to be introduced to computers as soon as he shows some interest. And just as your tod-

dler clambers onto your lap when you pick up a book or magazine or newspaper to read, he will probably be right at your elbow and eager to take part while you are sitting in front of the computer. Some children, mesmerized by the colors and sounds that the computer emits, exhibit interest in the machine as early as two or even younger.

Before two years of age, a child's ability to manipulate a computer may be limited to hitting keys at random or just sitting and watching the images on the screen. But this should not be taken to mean that the youngster should be excluded from the activity. Simply observing the changing shapes, colors, patterns and sounds produced by the computer can provide an infant or young child with all the pleasure and sensory awakening of an elaborate activity box.

Beginning at about the age of two, many children will use the computer readily and are able to acquire some basic skills through the machine. Your youngster can learn simple number and letter identification from an adult word-processing program; however, there are special children's software programs that teach those concepts and others in a fashion that many children will find far more entertaining and enjoyable.

Many programs use animated objects and characters, sounds or voices, music and vibrant colors to hold the child's interest. For example, a math learning game, which teaches a child to recognize numbers and to count, may show a group of animated objects on the screen while displaying the corresponding number.

Programs to prepare your youngster for reading may employ similar graphics to help the child identify letters of the alphabet and distinguish upper- and lower-case letters. And eye-catching graphics are standard in programs that are designed to expand a youngster's creative senses — programs that ask him to discriminate among particular colors or shapes, match objects to their names, or scribble or draw.

As your youngster grows in ability, he can hone his new skills with more advanced programs. Playing adventure games will broaden his imagination and problem-solving talents through role playing and the reasoning out of challenging situations.

By the age of five or six, a child may be able to do simple addition and subtraction, play spelling games and write little stories. Research has shown that youngsters with access to a computer often write with greater willingness and facility than do children who do not have access to a computer.

The still-developing coordination of children in this age group tends to make writing with a pencil a slow and arduous process, especially when there are corrections that must be made or rewriting that must be done. Using a computer helps your child put down his ideas quickly, and it also helps him organize his thoughts more easily. Later, the youngster can practice his penmanship by copying the story onto paper.

Equipping Your Computer

Although there are many software programs available that are designed specifically for children, not all of these programs will be suitable for your youngster. Even though a program is labeled for his age group, it may not be appropriate for your child's particular stage of development. In addition to following the tips on choosing software in the box below, you might also let your child help make the selections.

You and your youngster often can try out a program at your local library or in the store before you decide to purchase it. That way you will be able to gauge how your child reacts to the program's content and see whether he has any difficulty entering information into the computer.

A small child's limited manual dexterity may prevent him from responding quickly enough to the commands of some computer software programs. You should look for programs that do not demand swift reflexes but instead allow a young player plenty of time to make his selections.

Your child may find it advantageous to circumvent the computer keyboard altogether and employ another form of input device, something that is more easily manipulated by a child's small hands. One such instrument is a joystick — a handle that, when moved by your youngster, translates those movements into action on the computer screen. Also available are light pens and similar mechanisms that transfer marks the child makes on the screen's surface, or on a touch-sensitive tablet, onto the computer screen. Some computers come already equipped with these special input devices, but for other models they are accessories that must be purchased separately.

Whatever software or input system you choose, be sure that your computer is set up to accept it. If, for example, you select a program that includes a synthesized voice, your computer may need to be fitted with a special adapter.

Encouraging Computer Activities

Time spent at a computer is not only an excellent learning experience for your child, it can also provide a wonderful opportunity for you and your youngster to spend time together. Until he becomes familiar with the computer and the program, your child will probably need help loading the software, using the keyboard or other input device, such as a joystick, and understanding the program's instructions.

Throughout the hours that you and your child spend in front of the computer, your youngster will look to you for guidance and encouragement, and for interesting new ideas and help with problem solving.

It is important, however, not to rush your youngster into using a computer. Some children are simply not as intrigued by the machine as others, and they should not be pressured into playing with it or achieving a certain level of competence. To benefit and learn from a computer, your child must show an interest and be allowed to set his own pace. Before the age of six, a youngster's attention span is short — usually only five to 15 minutes — and if he is forced to continue beyond his personal tolerance level, he may develop an aversion to the whole business. Encourage your child to enjoy the computer and become familiar with it, but do not let it become the be-all and end-all of his play and learning. Treat it as just another everyday activity in his full and exciting life.

Choosing Suitable Software for Your Child

In shopping for children's computer programs, look for those that:

- emphasize basic skills, such as counting, guessing, matching, identifying.

- make learning fun by featuring appealing stories or characters, bright colors or interesting sounds instead of tedious drill routines.

- have simple goals and few rules.

- combine various ability levels so that a youngster can progress.

- offer the child help when she has difficulty responding to a question.

- move slowly enough so that she has time to think a problem through.

- are easy to operate and do not require a high level of manual dexterity or the use of both hands simultaneously to enter information.

- permit several choices rather than a single correct answer and avoid criticizing wrong answers.

- involve more than one player, to encourage cooperative effort and add to the fun.

Hand and Finger Dexterity

Even as very small babies, children seem to understand that their hands are something special. They will study them with fascination, carefully examining fingers, nails, palms and wrists. Soon they move on to grasping objects, developing techniques for grabbing everything from daddy's nose to kitty's tail. From there, it is a relatively short reach to mastery of the thousand and one activities that give a youngster a sense of control over her immediate environment.

By the time your child is one year old, she may be able to hold a crayon securely and scribble on a piece of paper. In another year, she may snip the edge of a piece of paper with scissors, and when she is three, she may have the skills to cut the paper in half. At five or six, she will be able to tie her own shoelaces, button buttons, and perhaps even sew with yarn and a large needle she has triumphantly threaded herself.

Such small muscle, or fine motor, skills seem simple to the adult who has been practicing them for decades, but in fact, they are exquisitely complex, requiring the integrated action of muscle and mind. Consider, for example, what is involved in playing Roll a Ball *(below)*. Before your youngster can consistently catch the ball and return it to you, she must learn to judge in which direction it is moving and how fast, when it will reach her, what she must do with her arms, wrists, hands and fingers to stop it, and how much force she must apply with each set of muscles and ligaments to send it back.

Eventually, the coordination involved in executing such movements becomes second nature, a sort of muscle memory. But to arrive at that confident state, your youngster has to work at it regularly, discovering through trial and error what her hands and fingers can and cannot accomplish. The activities on these two pages are aimed at developing manual dexterity in young children; a number of art and sculpture projects that also exercise fine motor skills can be found on pages 110-111. Whatever games and activities you choose, the objective should always be to build self-esteem and a sense of competence, as well as pure physical skill. Allow your youngster to proceed at her own rate and be sure to be generous in your praise when she succeeds, however imperfectly.

Pat-a-Cake   ages 9 months to 2 years

This is an age-old clapping game for the very young that promotes eye-hand coordination and body awareness. Because it includes three different hand movements that must be completed in specific order, the game also helps develop a child's comprehension of time sequences.

Hold your youngster's forearms and move them so that his hands clap to the rhythm of that old nonsense rhyme, "Pat-a-cake, pat-a-cake, baker man, make me a cake as fast as you can." When you get to the next line, "Roll it and roll it," move his hands in a circular motion. Finish the play with the phrase, "And stamp it with a *B* — and that will be enough for baby and me!" while at the same time gently slapping his hands on his knees or on the table to simulate stamping. Maintain eye contact with your youngster and smile at him to reassure him that this is something enjoyable to do. Before long, he will spontaneously join you in the game, trying to perform each of the gestures on his own. You can get greater value from the clapping gesture if you encourage him to clap on other occasions, such as after he has done something well and has earned praise for it.

Roll a Ball   ages 1 to 2

Sit on the floor, facing your child with your legs spread apart. Use a soft, six- to eight-inch rubber ball and roll it toward her open legs. Ask her to roll it back to you. If she hesitates, unsure of what she is supposed to do, say "Roll the ball to Mommy. I will roll it to you again." As she gains in skill, increase the speed of the roll and the distance between you. Talk to her as you make adjustments, using words such as "faster," "slower," "nearer," "farther," to help her develop simple time and space concepts. You can make the activity more interesting by asking her to roll the ball

into a fixed goal, such as an open box laid on its side. This activity stimulates small muscle control as well as offering an early lesson in the kinds of give and take children must learn before they can play most group games.

Windup Toys   ages 1 to 4

Toys that operate by means of a key that must be turned, a button that must be pushed or a bar that must be slid encourage your youngster to think about cause and effect while teaching finger and hand control. Such toys include windup trains, autos, buses and trucks, mechanical animals and people, and that old favorite, the jack-in-the-box. For the jack-in-the-box, set the toy before your toddler and, after winding the key and popping the clown in and out of his box a few times, ask her, "Where's Jack? Where did he go? Can you get him back?" Place the box within the child's reach and, if needed, put her hand on the crank. When the head pops up, say "Well, here he is. You found him." The two of you can take turns doing this little exercise so long as she enjoys it. You can play the same sort of game with a windup train, or some other rolling toy, by sending the train across the floor to your child and having her wind it up and send it back to you.

Hit the Target   ages 2 to 4

This version of ring toss or horseshoes, modified to suit a small child's level of competence, involves throwing a bean bag into a line-up of different-size pots, pans and other containers. Ask your youngster to kneel down a few feet away from the containers and suggest that he toss the bag into one of them. As he improves, you can encourage him to be more selective in his targets: "Let's see you get the bag into the biggest pot. That was perfect." Or if he misses, "That was very close."

You can make the game more interesting by taking turns and keeping score. Cheer when he succeeds, and ask him to help you by cheering when you hit the target. Not only will this game enhance your child's eye-hand coordination, it will teach the youngster such social skills as winning and losing gracefully, taking turns and cheering for others.

Building Blocks   ages 2 to 6

Blocks are among the best and most versatile of toys for your toddler. Many parents find it useful to buy a basic set by the time their child reaches two years of age, and to add more sets as his games and projects grow in complexity. A good basic set would include perhaps a dozen or more blocks of various sizes and shapes. You can begin by showing your child how to line up the blocks to form an imaginary train. Then demonstrate how you make a stack of two or three blocks. Discuss shapes and sizes: "Can you find me a long block? Where's the little round block? Here's a nice fat block." As you go along, you can make up stories to help him see the blocks as things with which to build: "Let's make a very long train. Now, show me how you can make the train shorter." Or, "Can you build a tall tower? Can you make it fall down?" As time goes on, your youngster can graduate to constructing whole castles and other buildings of his own imagining.

Manipulating blocks not only helps your youngster advance in eye-hand coordination, it teaches him the rudiments of such physical principles as balance and gravity. Children learn to plan ahead as well, and they gain valuable experience in selectivity — picking the right block for the right job. Moreover, block play helps youngsters become familiar with such concepts as shape, size and dimension.

Early Puzzles   ages 2 to 6

There are degrees of complexity to suit every age, but all puzzles exercise the same basic skills — manual dexterity, spatial perception and visual-spatial memory. Start with a very simple puzzle, perhaps consisting of nothing more than three or four large pieces. One sort of beginner puzzle requires your youngster to drop pieces representing such familiar things as a cow, an airplane or a hat into matching cutouts on a puzzle board. Another type consists of pieces that do not so much interlock as nest loosely together. Show your child how the puzzle looks when it is assembled, then spread the pieces apart, keeping them in the same arrangement. Ask him to put the pieces back together. When the youngster succeeds, you can make the puzzle a bit more challenging: "How would it be if I mixed up the pieces a little? Do you think you can put them where they belong?" While you are doing the puzzle, talk about the pieces in a way that helps your child see their differences: "This one is round on one side. Where does it go? Where do you suppose this one with the squiggly edge will fit?"

As his skills advance, introduce him to more complicated interlocking puzzles. Say to your youngster, "This might be too hard to do, but let's give it a try anyway." This will lessen the pressure to succeed and offer him an opportunity to reach beyond his current level of proficiency.

Stringing Beads   ages 3 to 5

Here is a hands-and-fingers activity that produces something a child can wear herself or give to you, which is a nice way for her to build confidence and win approval. Give your youngster a long colored shoelace, knotted at one end, and an assortment of wooden beads, large-holed buttons, spools and other suitable items. Let her play with them for a while until she is familiar with the parts. Then, ask the child to hold the shoelace, threading end up, and say, "Look, I'm going to take this big yellow bead and put it on the shoelace. Here it goes . . . all the way to the bottom. Do you want to put the next bead on? Which one would you like to put on the shoelace?" After your child has finished stringing all the items — it may take several play sessions — tie the ends together to make a necklace.

If your youngster enjoys this activity, you can vary it by asking her to string beads that match in color, shape or size, or that have a repeating pattern. You should be sure, of course, to remind your youngster that bead parts must not go in her mouth and to have her remove the necklace when she is playing active games or before she takes a nap. ∴

Group Games

Group games strengthen your child's developing skills in jumping, skipping, running, leaping and balance, but perhaps their most important long-term benefit is in teaching the basic tools of social behavior. In group games, a youngster experiences the excitement of competition, the triumph of winning, the challenge of devising a strategy and the virtues of cooperating with others to achieve a common goal. She also begins to understand that many desirable activities are accompanied by rules that must be followed.

Some of the games on these pages can be played by children as young as two, but group games are generally most successful for youngsters older than three, the age at which most children are ready to absorb instructions and remember rules. However, you may find that some children cannot yet cope with the temporary anxiety of being tagged out or of playing a lone adversarial role as It. Such children need extra support and encouragement when they play, and you may even wish to intercede gently from time to time, stretching the rules to give the persistent loser an opportunity to win. In games where strategy plays a part, you can suggest that it is a good idea to plan ahead; in hide-and-seek, for example, you might say, "Look for a hiding place that is dark, where It will have a hard time seeing you."

A natural time for group games is at a birthday party, but any occasion that brings several youngsters together is fine. Keep each game fairly short in order to prevent the group from losing its enthusiasm. And keep the mood fun rather than hotly competitive. When someone is designated It and is pitted against the rest, make an effort to play enough rounds to give everyone a chance at both roles. In team games, shuffle the children around to make teams as nearly even as possible, and encourage players to be supportive of their teammates — even when they make mistakes — and tolerant of their opponents. A number of organized games, such as soccer and T-ball, are played at community centers and youth groups. Formal sports at this time can be highly motivating to some children but can result in too much tension for others. If your youngster participates in these activities, emphasize team spirit and group play skills such as listening to instructions and following rules.

Follow the Leader   ages 2 to 5

This old favorite helps youngsters practice their physical coordination while having fun together. Start by choosing a leader, and have everyone else form a straight line behind him. Invite the leader to take the line forward by making some movement — hopping on one foot or walking on tiptoes — and ask the others to follow the leader. Let the leader change movements several times, then choose another leader. Young children can play this game successfully if the movements are kept simple. Older children are likely to improvise more, to challenge themselves and their friends with more difficult movements. Older children also take particular pleasure in being the leader and having the opportunity to show off without fear of criticism.

Obstacle Course   ages 2 to 6

One of the nice things about obstacle course is that it can be played by children of different ages simply by adjusting the obstacles to suit the skills of the group. Ask the children to help you think of things to put in a path that they must navigate. In the house, this might be cardboard boxes open at both ends, a line of milk cartons or a pile of cushions. Outdoors you can make use of ropes, rubber tires, a bench or even a tree. As you set up the game, keep in mind such movements as jumping off, jumping into, crawling over, stepping off and climbing through. Go over the course with the children and change it often to keep it interesting. Ask the children to suggest changes and talk with them about which obstacles they find fun, challenging or silly. This game strengthens the arm and leg muscles and improves climbing, crawling and jumping skills as well as balance. Your youngster also learns about sequencing as she remembers the order in which the path is laid out. And, of course, the more creative the child is in finding obstacles, the better time she and her playmates will have.

Hide-and-Seek   ages 2 to 6

With younger children, you may wish to play this game indoors where you can keep a closer eye on things. Older children will find hide-and-seek great fun either indoors or outdoors. The game is to hide oneself from the person chosen as It. Hide-and-seek is a natural outgrowth of the "Where's baby? . . .

There he is!" games that so delight infants and toddlers.

Choose one of the children as the first It. Have him stand at home base — a tree, a chair or some other place relatively clear of obstructions — cover his eyes and count to 10. For younger children you can do the counting; for older children you might raise the count to 20. At the same time, send the other players off to hide. When It reaches the end of his count, he shouts "Here I come, ready or not!" He then begins to search high and low for the hidden children. Each time the child who is It finds a hidden child, he calls out the discovery — "I see Johnny under the bush!" and races back to tag home base, which renders Johnny out. If you wish to discourage running in the house, an indoor player can be counted out as soon as he is discovered. The last child to be found becomes the next It. You can help younger children get started by giving them little hints on where to hide or where It might start looking.

For older children, the game of hide-and-seek can be made more challenging by giving hiding players the possibility of getting set free and freeing other out, or captured, players, too. This can be done when a discovered child manages to beat It back to home base and shouts "All home free." The game then starts over again, with the original It repeating his search for the other children a second time.

Hide-and-seek improves coordination and running skills while rewarding a child's ability to be observant and to find good hiding places. The more complex version of the game also challenges the youngster who is It to juggle the conflicting needs of protecting home base while finding other hidden children, which is a gentle introduction to the valuable art of establishing priorities and taking risks.

Red Light-Green Light   ages 3 to 6
Although red light-green light can be played in a large room, it is basically an active outdoor game for any number of children — the more the merrier. The idea is to move without being caught. Ask the children to line up and face It, who is five to 10 yards away. Now, It turns her back on the others and calls "green light — one, two, three." The others move forward as It is calling, but they must stop on the count of three — because at three, It will call out "red light," spin around and look to see if any of the players are still running. Whoever is spotted moving then becomes the new It. If one of the children playing the game gets close enough to tag It when she is not looking, the game breaks up into a tag match, and the first person to be tagged by It is the new It. You can add variation to the game by having the children tiptoe instead of run, or by asking them to hop or to skip. The game called red light-green light helps develop body control and teaches youngsters the virtues of listening carefully and following rules.

Shadow Tag   ages 4 to 6
Your child's natural fascination with shadows can be turned into a game that gives form to his play. Explain to the players that the object of the game is to keep away from the person who is It. The It, for his part, tries his best to step on or tag his friends' shadows; when he succeeds, he changes places with the child whose shadow has been tagged and that child becomes It. The game then starts all over again. You can begin by walking the children through a game or two of shadow tag until they understand the rules; you might, for example, take the role of It yourself the first time to show the youngsters how the game works — and to show them that It is not such a bad thing to be. Give hints in the beginning that It is getting closer or farther from a player's shadow. Once the children get the hang of the game, you can vary the rounds to make it more interesting; you might suggest that the youngsters hop, jump, slide, or fly with their arms outstretched instead of walking.

The game of shadow tag helps youngsters improve such large muscle skills as running, skipping and turning. It also enhances the children's awareness of such spatial concepts as "near" and "far," and the game may even vent natural feelings of aggression in a harmless way.

Statues   ages 4 to 6
The object of this game is to get children to assume various positions and to hold them just like a statue — that is, to remain motionless no matter what. At the same time, another player, designated It, is doing his best to make the others laugh or move, by making funny faces at the statues, running around them and doing anything else he can think of short of touching them in order to break their concentration. The first child to laugh or move becomes the next It and the game starts over again. Once the children have learned the game, they can assume all sorts of positions — standing on one foot, bending over, stretching out their arms, whatever happens to strike their fancy. Playing statues challenges a youngster's ability to control his body and his emotions. And the game also teaches children an appreciation of laughter and of the ridiculous. ∴

Balance and Coordination

As soon as your youngster has mastered walking, he is in his own mind ready to take on the world. But in truth, he still has a very limited sense of his body's abilities. His large, or gross motor, muscles, with which he moves his arms, legs, head and torso, seldom perform as the child wishes and expects, because he has not yet learned enough about balance, eye-muscle coordination, or the relationship between muscle effort and results.

You can help your child unravel these mysteries in a variety of entertaining and challenging ways. The chances are that he will enjoy all of the exercises and games described below. But if he shows clear signs of disliking or fearing any one of them, quickly move on to something else; you can try the activity in question some other time. Nor is there any need to stress perfection at this stage; instead, emphasize the fun of discovering what his muscles can do. When introducing tumbling exercises, you will want to guide him gently through the steps at first to prevent injury. Be sure, too, that the room or play area is safe and suitable for each activity; use a foam pad or a mattress to cushion falls, and move sharp-edged furniture well out of the way so that even the most exuberant youngster cannot run into trouble.

It is a good idea to include opportunities for flexing, stretching and strengthening large muscles daily. You may wish to begin with warm-ups, which contribute to body tone and coordination in their own right. By making these exercises a natural part of your child's day, you are helping to lay the foundation for a lifetime of fitness. As your youngster learns that he can control his body and use it in more and more exciting ways — that he can run fast and jump high, that he can wiggle and climb and do a somersault with aplomb — his self-esteem rises and he gains the internal reserves to go out and meet new challenges.

If you are thinking about introducing him to formal gymnastic or other athletic lessons, bear in mind that some children thrive in a class under the tutelage of a professional teacher, but some preschoolers do not adapt well to such an atmosphere. If you do choose to start formal lessons, you will want to be sure that your youngster is ready, that he thinks they are fun and does not feel pressured to compete.

Giddy-Up Horsie   ages 2 to 3

Young children like nothing better than riding around on their mommy or daddy's back, both because they like being physically close and because they find the higher vantage point new and exciting. And surely there is something wonderful, too, in the sense of control your youngster feels over his submissive steed. To play the game, get down on your hands and knees and have your child climb on your back. A toddler may need another adult's help in getting aboard. Be sure that he has a firm grip on your shirt and will not fall off. Ask, "Where would you like to go?" and then crawl around as requested. Another time, pretend that you are a big dog, a lion or an elephant. Enhance the fun with barks and other suitable sounds. Many youngsters delight in hearing about an imaginary landscape they are traveling through: "We are going through a great big jungle. There's a bright red parrot over there. Can you imagine how its call sounds?" Giddy-up horsie will improve your child's sense of balance as well as exercise his imagination.

Hoops   ages 2 to 4

An old bicycle tire or hula hoop will be perfect for this game. Lay the hoop on the ground and ask your youngster to step in and out of it, using first one foot at a time, then hopping out with one foot and finally, jumping out of the hoop with both feet. You can vary the game by having your child walk around inside the hoop until you clap your hands or sing, then he can hop or jump out and continue walking on the outside of the hoop until you give the signal to switch again. This simple game strengthens leg muscles and improves coordination, while teaching your youngster to follow instructions.

Tunnels   ages 2 to 4

Youngsters can find adventure as well as good exercise in pretend tunnels and caves. You can get your child started in this activity by taking a large cardboard carton, opening the ends and taping them flat against the sides for greater sturdiness. Lay the cardboard tunnel on the floor and ask your child to go through on his stomach, pulling himself along with his arms. When he has emerged from the tunnel, you might ask him if he would like to wiggle through like a snake or push through on his back. You should encourage the youngster to invent his own ways of moving through the tunnel.

You can vary the activity by joining two or more cartons of different sizes together and setting them off at slight angles so that your young explorer has to make a turn or two during his travels. On another occasion, you might wish to make a low table into a cave by draping a sheet over two sides of the table and sending your child through the other openings. Besides helping your youngster practice muscle control, this activity develops spatial awareness and depth perception.

Jump Over the Stream   ages 2 to 4

Score two parallel lines on the ground, or set out parallel lengths of string or tape on the floor, separating them at first only by a couple of inches. Ask your youngster to imagine that she is standing on the edge of a stream. Then, ask her if she can hop across the stream without falling in. If she misses — by stepping on or inside the lines — you can pretend that she is wet and dry her off briskly with an imaginary towel. When the child succeeds in jumping across, ask if she thinks she can jump across a wider stream. Show your youngster that by swinging her arms she can increase her distance.

Continue to move the lines apart, making the stream into a little river, a bigger river, then a mighty river, until you see that your youngster is nearing her physical limit. Try to end this jumping game on a positive note, so that she makes her last leap a successful one. Jump over the stream is an entertaining way for your child to improve her hopping, jumping and coordination skills. The youngster will also learn to assess distances and alter her muscle effort accordingly.

Balancing Acts   ages 2 to 6

You can help your child develop confidence in his sense of balance by encouraging him to practice balancing on a variety of safe surfaces. All kinds of things will serve the purpose for this activity: the section lines in the sidewalk, the low curb along a quiet street, the pattern in the kitchen linoleum floor, the edge of the living-room rug. Or you can draw a chalk line on the driveway or lay down a two-by-eight-inch plank in the backyard or in the playroom.

Suggest to your youngster that a good way to keep his balance at first is to walk with his arms outstretched to the sides. As he becomes proficient at balancing forward, encourage him to try walking backwards, sideways, heel-to-toe. Children as young as two can begin learning to walk a straight line. Older children may enjoy pretending that they are circus performers walking a balance beam you have set up a few inches off the ground. Balancing helps coordinate large muscles with information being gathered by the eyes and inner ears, and it is essential to all other large motor activities. As soon as your youngster gains confidence in his ability to keep his equilibrium under different circumstances, he will be ready to begin to take the risks required to learn bicycling, skating and such.

Catching   ages 3 to 6

This game develops timing and finely tuned eye-hand coordination. You can start your youngster off with a brightly colored balloon, which will float down so slowly that she will have considerable time to prepare to catch it. You can show her how by catching the balloon yourself at first, explaining that the way to catch something is to "make a basket with your hands." Now, face her at a distance of three feet or so and toss the balloon into the air so that it floats down within easy reach. Say, "Here it comes. Get your arms ready to catch the balloon"; or "Daddy is going to throw the balloon up high. Can you catch it before it touches the ground?" As she progresses, encourage her to throw the balloon back to you. When she is adept at balloon play, you can introduce her to medium-size spongy rubber balls, then balls of smaller size that she can bounce and catch on her own.

Front Roll   ages 4 to 6

Explain to your child that you are going to teach her to roll, just like a ball. Show her how to tuck in her chin to her chest to prevent hurting herself; if necessary, have her hold something soft between chin and chest to help her remember. Then, have her bend over with arms stretched down until her hands touch the ground. Now, place one of your hands at the back of her neck and the other hand on her upper thigh, and begin to talk her through the roll. "Lean forward while I hold you. Put your chin down tight and let your head touch the ground in front of you. It's all right, I've got you." Guide her in a gradual roll, encouraging her to stay tucked like a ball until her legs come around and she is in a sitting position. Rolling heightens body awareness and large motor control, while giving your youngster experience in putting instructions to use. Rolling also teaches about changing perceptions as her world momentarily turns upside down.

Crab Walk   ages 4 to 6

Ask your child to lie on her back on a carpeted surface, with her knees bent upward and her feet planted squarely on the floor. Have her put her hands flat on the floor on either side of her chest. Now, ask the youngster to lift her body and head off the floor. You may need to give a gentle boost under her shoulders or her bottom the first couple of times. Once the child is up, ask her to move around the room like a crab. Getting arms and legs working together can be a bit difficult at first, so she may need some suggestions from you. Once your youngster has mastered moving forward, ask her to show you other directions: backwards, sideways, diagonally. Ask her to tell you how it feels to be a crab. The crab walk helps strengthen arm, leg and stomach muscles, while improving balance and coordination. It is a playful precursor to the kinds of exercises older children will be taught in school fitness programs. ⁘

Swimming

Swimming ranks as one of the most healthful and satisfying of all physical activities, one that will serve your child well throughout his lifetime. Not only is swimming relaxing and refreshing, it helps tone virtually every skeletal muscle in the body. When practiced regularly, swimming also exercises and strengthens the heart and lungs. What is more, skill in swimming will open up a range of pleasurable social activities that your youngster can enjoy for many years. You can introduce him to water play when he is three to six months of age. By the time he is a toddler, he can begin to learn the fundamentals of floating and propelling himself through the water; by four or five he may be able to swim on his own.

Your baby's bath is a natural place to start. Make it fun, with plenty of time for splashing about. If you have a yard, consider including a plastic wading pool for your toddler's summer pleasure. Introduce your youngster to water gradually, and stay with the simplest activities until he is ready to move on. If you are already a water enthusiast, he is likely to absorb some of your confidence. If you have anxieties, you may wish to spend some time getting more comfortable yourself before joining your impressionable child in water play.

Some parents may wish to enroll their child in an organized swim program at the local Y or school. The best programs stress safety and familiarity with the water over technical skills. Before enrolling, you should satisfy yourself that a qualified instructor trained in CPR is in charge; that children are taught on a one-to-one basis, preferably with a parent as partner; that forced submersion is prohibited; that all participants shower before class; and that all children still wearing diapers be required to wear plastic training pants to guard against transmission of common intestinal infections.

As your child grows older, you may wish to join a neighborhood swimming pool where he can put some of his more ambitious activities into practice. Make sure the pool you choose is suitable: For a youngster's comfort and safety, water temperature should be at least 85° F., noise and confusion minimal, and high standards of hygiene consistently followed. Wherever your child swims, remember that nothing can absolutely waterproof a youngster; you should never relax your vigilance when children and water mix.

Motor Boat   ages 2 to 6

Sit in the water, holding your child so that both of you have your heads just above the surface. Tell her that you are going to be a pretend motor boat, then put your mouth under the water and blow bubbles. Invite your child to join in the fun as you blow more bubbles. Keep constant eye contact with her and smile when you stop bubbling.

After a couple of submersions, ask your youngster what kind of boat she would like to pretend to be. A speedboat, perhaps, or an ocean liner or a submarine? Bubble blowing gives your child practice in getting her face wet while at the same time introducing the idea of exhaling under water. The youngster will also take pleasure in the noise play.

Ring-around-the-Rosy   ages 3 to 6

A wet version of the universally popular childhood game, this activity is a first step for your child in acquiring confidence under water. Hold the youngster either in your arms or by both hands — the choice depends on age — in water that is roughly as high as his chest. Circle around as you start to sing, "Ring around the rosy, a pocketful of posies, ashes, ashes. . ." When you get to the last line of the jingle, "We all fall down!" bend your knees so that you submerge more of yourselves. As your child's confidence grows, gradually dip lower and lower. Teach him to close his mouth and hold his breath each time you go through a dip. Eventually — if not the first day you play, then some days hence — you should both be able to go completely under water.

Splashing Games   ages 2 to 6

Some children are afraid of getting their faces wet, and this fear is a great handicap in learning to swim. You can help alleviate your youngster's anxiety by playing simple splashing games with her while she is still very young.

Begin by encouraging her to splash and have fun as she sits in a wading pool. First, use your own arms to splash water while saying, "Look how high the water is going. There's water everywhere. Can you make it splash, too?" Then show her how to splash her arms and legs against the water. Encourage her to do it again, on her own this time.

Try this variation when she graduates to a bigger pool: As she stands facing you in water up to her chest, toss a large rubber ball in the air so that when it falls it splashes both of you. Smile and say, "We're all wet! That was fun! Let's do it again." Encourage her to toss the ball so that it splashes only you. Again, show her that you think the game is fun.

Still another way to have fun getting wet is by playing a game you can call "table-tennis ball chase." Drop a table-tennis ball in front of her and ask her to blow it in your direction. She will have to get her mouth down near water level, a necessary first step in submerging her face. And it will give her a start on controlling her breathing while in the water.

Kick, Kick, Kick   ages 2 to 6
This activity will give your youngster an early lesson in moving through the water under her own power. Stand in chest-high water and hold your child under the arms so that she is floating on her stomach with her face toward you. Encourage her to kick her legs, saying, "Kick, kick, kick," and talk to her about what she is doing: "Now, you are doing a nice slow kick, now fast, now slow again. Look at all the waves that you are making!" Once your youngster has the idea of kicking down, you can ask her to add bubble blowing. The combination of breathing and locomotion will give her an idea of true swimming, and your child will get a wonderful sense of her ability to affect her environment when she sees and hears how much commotion she is able to create in the water.

Doggie Paddle   ages 4 to 6
You can complete your youngster's introduction to the basic components of swimming with this activity, which focuses on the use of arms and legs. Stand at the shallow end of the pool and hold your child so that she is floating in a horizontal position with her head toward the edge of the pool and her feet braced against your thighs. Ask her to move her arms to swim to the pool steps or ladder when you count to three and, on signal, move her in the right direction, supporting her as she paddles her arms. Ask her to hold her breath as you repeat the gliding exercise. When she has the arm movement mastered and can consistently remember to hold her breath, shift your position to the side so that her legs are freed. Now, with one hand under her stomach for support, ask her to kick as well. At some point, you will find that arm and leg motion is sufficient to keep her afloat and propel her forward, and you can withdraw your hand support after she starts paddling and kicking.

You can increase the challenge for your youngster by moving farther from the pool edge so that the child must swim a greater distance. And you can make a game of her progress by counting

the strokes each time. Your youngster will feel as if she is really swimming as you count higher and higher and she is impressed by the distance she is traveling. Follow along with your child and be ready to offer support quickly if she falters. The confidence and coordination that your child requires to be consistently successful at swimming may take awhile to develop.

Walk the Wall   ages 4 to 6
This activity teaches a child to hold onto the edge of the pool if he falls in or gets too tired to paddle. Stand in the water holding your child under the arms so that he is facing the pool wall and within reach of it. Ask him to hold the top edge with his hands and to put his feet against the wall. Let go of the child briefly, and say, "Good for you! You are holding on all by yourself!" Next, you might want to ask the child to walk the wall, using his hands and toes. You can show your youngster how he can move to the left and right by moving his hands and feet in either direction.

As your child gains coordination, encourage him to walk a certain distance in one direction, then the other. Suggest that he try doing it with his hands alone, and say, "I bet no one will ever believe you could walk on a wall without using your feet! This is fun!" The youngster will gain a sense of his body's buoyancy as he goes along the pool wall, and the activity will reduce anxiety about being in deep water.

Jumping In   ages 4 to 6
Some children are afraid of entering the water in any way except by wading in the shallow end. This activity teaches your youngster to enter the pool from all sides. Ask you child to sit or stand on the edge of the pool while you stand in shoulder-high water facing her. Reach up and hold her hands and ask her to jump. Reassure her that you will catch her and hold her up. Then, gently pull your child into the water with you. Do not let her head go under until you have completed the exercise several times and she shows that she is ready to be submerged. Prepare for the dunking by saying, "This time we are going to let you go under water, but I will still have your hands. Remember to hold your breath." As your child gets better at this, you can have her jump while you hold one of her hands and finally, by herself. Children who get used to entering the pool in water over their heads are less likely to panic if they accidentally fall into the water. ⁂

Dance

From their earliest days, children show a spontaneous inclination to move their bodies to the rhythmic sounds of music. Later, when youngsters learn to walk, more purposeful activities such as marching, dancing and creative movement become possible. You can play an important role in developing this potential in your child and at the same time promote her physical coordination and self-expression.

Begin when she is an infant by exposing her to many kinds of music — from modern jazz and country-western to waltzes and marches — each with its distinctive sounds, rhythms and moods. Dance with your child, holding her close so she can experience the pleasures of moving to a bouncy beat, a fast beat, a slow and languorous beat. Once she is able to navigate on her own, you can hold her hands and, using your own body as an example, help her discover how she can become an active part of the music by moving her torso from side to side and by moving her feet in different steps. With encouragement, children often begin to step around to music by the age of two, and by three they can follow simple instructions.

As your child shows that she is ready, use rhythmic movement to develop strength and coordination. Marching in step with others is a particularly useful activity for this, and it has the added bonus of teaching cooperative play. Introduce your youngster to the creative use of movement to express imagination: "Let's be a bird," or "Let's be a leaf in the wind." If you ask her to show you a sad dance, a mad dance or a happy-birthday dance, she will learn how she can use her body to express emotion as well. At first, you will have to provide the music and ideas, but look for opportunities to let her take the lead in choosing music and defining her dance. A few simple musical noisemakers such as drums, bells, tambourines or shakers will enhance a youngster's pleasure and involvement.

In many communities, dance classes for preschoolers are available. But it is probably better for you to teach your youngster to move freely to the music before beginning formal lessons, which tend to emphasize set steps and routines. Dance at this age should be a source of uninhibited joy and discovery, and those pleasures can best be experienced at home with a loving parent.

Rhythmic Movement ages 4 to 8 months

Your child does not have to be able to walk in order to enjoy music and rhythmic movement. When he is just a few months old, you can introduce him to music and dance by playing your favorite tunes or singing a song while holding his hands and moving them to the tempo. He will get a direct introduction to these pleasures by feeling the different ways you move his arms as the music progresses.

Jiggle-Giggle ages 2 to 4

Choose one of your child's favorite songs as rhythmic background. Have her stand opposite you and ask her to jiggle whatever part of the body you call out. Then, call out one by one, "your arm," "your two knees," "your foot" and so forth, allowing perhaps 10 seconds for each body part, as both you and your youngster run through this musical anatomy lesson. Begin with the most common anatomical words and gradually introduce such things as "thigh," "calf" and "elbow." To vary the game, you could change the instructions from "jiggle" to "circle," "swing" or "touch."

Once your youngster understands how to play the game, encourage her to call out the parts of the body to jiggle. This activity should be completely uninhibited, even a little silly, and if the two of you get to giggling, so much the better. Along the way, your child will be learning movement, quick responsiveness to instructions and some new words.

Moving Like the Animals ages 2 to 6

If your youngster has been on a trip to the zoo, she has had an opportunity to observe a variety of animals in action. This humorous dance activity encourages the child to use her observations in an imaginative way and at the same time to explore her own body movements. You can begin by asking your youngster about her visit to the zoo: "Do you remember the elephant we saw at the zoo? Can you show me how it moves?"

If your youngster is puzzled about what to do at first, you can show her how to make an elephant's trunk with your arms and demonstrate a slow, lumbering gait. Help her show you some of the other animals she saw — the climbing monkey; the graceful gazelle; the low, slow turtle; the strutting ostrich. You can embellish the game by asking the youngster to imitate a fast animal, then a slow one, a big one and a little one; this will help teach her sequencing and the idea of contrasts.

Music, though not absolutely necessary, adds to the fun of this activity. Saint-Saëns' *Carnival of the Animals,* which may be available on loan from your local public library, is one good choice. Or as an alternative to zoo animals, you could play Prokofiev's *Peter and the Wolf* and suggest to your youngster that she imagine herself first as Peter, then as the cat, the duck, the wolf and the grandfather — and move as she imagines they would move at appropriate moments in the story.

Shadow Dancing   ages 3 to 5

This is an indoor activity, suitable for one or several children, depending on how much room you have available. It encourages spatial awareness and expressive body movements. Place a strong light — from a spotlight, a movie or slide projector, or some other lamp that sends a relatively narrow beam — so that it projects against a bare wall. Ask your youngster to dance back and forth across the beam so that her shadow is displayed on the wall where she can see it.

Encourage the youngster to experiment with different positions, to make her shadow larger or smaller, to hold herself upright like a straight line, to become a rectangle by bending down and touching the floor in front of her, or perhaps to make a triangle by touching her right foot to her left knee. You might want to hold your youngster's hand and dance along with her so that she sees your two shadows interacting.

Marching   ages 3 to 5

Your youngster can begin to march soon after she masters walking, and she will likely enjoy it with increasing proficiency throughout her preschool years. Begin by showing her that marching is done by bringing the knees up high while walking at a steady pace. Have your youngster follow you from room to room as both of you march. You can make up a little song as you parade: "We are marching, Mom and Kathie, left knee, right knee, left knee, right knee, march, march, march" — or something to this effect. When your youngster gets the idea, you can play some march music and add arm swinging to show her how to get her arms going in rhythmic opposition to her legs. Then you can add instruments — a piepan and a wooden spoon, or some other noisemaker that catches the child's fancy. Marching develops coordination in young children and makes learning "left" and "right" easier and more fun.

Feeling the Music   ages 3 to 6

Select a piece of music — preferably an instrumental rather than a vocal number, so that the beat will be easier to hear — and have your youngster dance to it. Start her off by asking how the music makes her feel. You might suggest, "This jazz makes me want to dance around in circles. What do your arms and legs want to do?" When you both have explored the first selection, try a second recording with a distinctly different tempo and see how she dances to it. This activity teaches your child to be aware of the rhythmic elements in different kinds of music and to respond with her own feelings and physical movements. You can enhance the game with a few props, such as a shawl or a scarf, that will move interestingly with your young dancer. If possible, you should set up the activity in a room equipped with a wall mirror, so that your child can see herself as she dances.

Clap Hands   ages 4 to 6

Learning about rhythm is a central part of dancing, and you can help your child get started by playing a simple piece of music and clapping your hands to the beat. Ask your child to join in when he also hears the beat. If he has trouble distinguishing the rhythm, hold his hands and clap the beat for him until he catches on. You can count "one, two, three, four, one, two, three, four . . ." to emphasize what you are hearing. Repeat the song and now add foot tapping to the hand clapping. This will develop his ability to listen to rhythms and anticipate them; it will also enhance his hand and foot coordination.

Sequencing   ages 5 to 6

This activity teaches a number of basic skills, including problem solving and remembering a series of ideas in a fixed order. It also helps your youngster develop the coordination necessary for running, skipping and balance.

Play some music with a variety of rich sounds, such as a polka or a samba, and tell your child that you would like his help in creating a new dance. Suggest some specific movements to include in the dance, such as, "I want a part that has skipping around in a circle, a part for going up and down, a running part and a part that has a zigzag shape to it." You should adjust the number of parts in the dance — or problems to solve and ideas to remember — to your child's level of maturity. When he has completed the dance invention, dance the parts with him as the two of you have created them. If the movements of his dance do not match the beat of the music, ask him how he could change them so they would match better. Vary the game at another time by asking the youngster to make up his own sequences and introduce his own parts. Or offer him a variety of music and ask him to make up new dances to music that he chooses. ⁝⁝

Bibliography

BOOKS

Ames, Louise Bates, and Joan Ames Chase, *Don't Push Your Preschooler.* New York: Harper & Row, 1980.

Anderson, Eugene, George Redman and Charlotte Rogers. *Self-Esteem for Tots to Teens.* New York: Meadowbrook, 1984.

Avery, Marie L., and Alice Higgins, *Help Your Child Learn How to Learn.* Englewood Cliffs, N.J.: Prentice-Hall, 1962.

Beck, Joan, *How to Raise a Brighter Child.* New York: Pocket Books, 1975.

Braga, Laurie, and Joseph Braga, *Learning and Growing: A Guide to Child Development.* Englewood Cliffs, N.J.: Prentice-Hall, 1975.

Brenner, Barbara, and Mari Endreweit, *Bank Street's Family Computer Book.* New York: Ballantine Books, 1984.

Brown, Janet F., ed., *Curriculum Planning for Young Children.* Washington: National Association for the Education of Young Children, 1982.

Brutten, Milton, Sylvia O. Richardson, M.D., and Charles Mangel, *Something's Wrong with My Child.* New York: Harcourt Brace Jovanovich, 1979.

Buchenholz, Gretchen, *Teach Your Child with Games.* New York: Simon & Schuster, 1984.

Burtt, Kent Garland, *Smart Times.* New York: Harper & Row, 1984.

Carroll, Lewis, *Alice's Adventures in Wonderland* and *Through the Looking-Glass.* New York: Macmillan, 1966.

Chance, Paul, *Learning Through Play.* New York: Gardner Press, 1979.

Cole, Ann, Carolyn Haas, Faith Bushnell and Betty Weinberger, *I Saw a Purple Cow and 100 Other Recipes for Learning.* Boston: Little, Brown, 1972.

Cummings, Rhoda Woods, and Cleborne D. Maddux, *Parenting the Learning Disabled.* Springfield, Ill.: Charles C. Thomas, 1985.

Cunningham, Cliff, and Patricia Sloper, *Helping Your Exceptional Baby.* New York: Pantheon Books, 1980.

DeLorenzo, Lorisa, and Robert John DeLorenzo, M.D., *Total Child Care: From Birth to Age Five.* Garden City, N.Y.: Doubleday, 1982.

De Villiers, Peter A., and Jill G. de Villiers, *Early Language.* Cambridge: Harvard University Press, 1979.

Diagram Group, *The Brain: A User's Manual.* New York: Berkley Books, 1983.

Dodson, Fitzhugh, *How to Parent.* New York: New American Library, 1970.

Elkind, David, *The Hurried Child: Growing Up Too Fast Too Soon.* Reading, Mass.: Addison-Wesley, 1981.

Foundation for Children with Learning Disabilities, *The FCLD Learning Disabilities Resource Guide.* New York: New York University Press, 1985.

Flavell, John H., *Cognitive Development.* Englewood Cliffs, N.J.: Prentice-Hall, 1985.

Glazer, Tom, *Do Your Ears Hang Low? Fifty More Musical Fingerplays.* Garden City, N.Y.: Doubleday, 1980.

Glover, John A., *A Parent's Guide to Intelligence Testing.* Chicago: Nelson Hall, 1979.

Gordon, Ira J., *Baby Learning Through Baby Play.* New York: St. Martin's, 1970.

Gordon, Ira J., Barry Guinagh and R. Emile Jester, *Child Learning Through Child Play.* New York: St. Martin's, 1972.

Grasselli, Rose N., and Priscilla A. Hegner, *Playful Parenting.* New York: Perigee Books, 1981.

Hall, Eleanor G., and Nancy Skinner, *Somewhere to Turn.* New York: Teachers College Press, 1980.

Hartman, Harriet, *Let's Play and Learn.* New York: Human Sciences Press, 1976.

Hayden, Alice H., et al., *Mainstreaming Preschoolers: Children with Learning Disabilities.* Washington: U.S. GPO, no date.

Hill, Dorothy M., *Mud, Sand, and Water.* Washington: National Association for the Education of Young Children, 1977.

Honig, Alice S., *Playtime Learning Games for Young Children.* Syracuse, N.Y.: Syracuse University Press, 1982.

Isenberg, Joan P., and Judith E. Jacobs, *Playthings As Learning Tools: A Parents' Guide.* New York: John Wiley & Sons, 1982.

Johnson, Doris J., "Psycho-Educational Evaluation of Children with Learning Disabilities: Study of Auditory Processes." In *Learning Disabilities and Related Disorders,* ed. by J. Gordon Millichap. Chicago: Year Book Medical Publishers, 1977.

Kagan, Jerome, *The Nature of the Child.* New York: Basic Books, 1984.

Kaufmann, Felice, *Your Gifted Child and You.* Reston, Va.: Council for Exceptional Children, 1976.

Kellogg, Rhoda, and Scott O'Dell, *The Psychology of Children's Art.* Del Mar, Calif.: CRM Inc., 1967.

Koste, Virginia Glasgow, *Dramatic Play in Childhood.* New Orleans: Anchorage Press, 1978.

Lasky, Lila, and Rose Mukerji, *Art: Basic for Young Children.* Washington: National Association for the Education of Young Children, 1980.

Licpman, Lise, *Your Child's Sensory World.* New York: Dial Press, 1973.

Lowenfeld, Viktor, and W. Lambert Brittain, *Creative and Mental Growth.* New York: Macmillan, 1975.

McCall, Robert B.:
Infants. Cambridge: Harvard University Press, 1979.
Programmed Learning Aid for Intelligence and Heredity. Homewood, Ill.: Learning Systems Company, 1975.

McDonald, Dorothy T., *Music in Our Lives: The Early Years.* Washington: National Association for the Education of Young Children, 1979.

Machado, Jeanne M., *Early Childhood Experiences in Language Arts.* Albany, N.Y.: Delmar Publishers, 1980.

Marzollo, Jean:
Superkids: Creative Learning Activities for Children 5-15. New York: Harper & Row, 1981.
Supertot: Creative Learning Activities for Children from One to Three and Sympathetic Advice for Their Parents. New York: Harper Colophon Books, 1977.

Marzollo, Jean, and Janice Lloyd, *Learning Through Play.* New York: Harper & Row, 1972.

Maynard, Fredelle, *Guiding Your Child to a More Creative Life.* Garden City, N.Y.: Doubleday, 1973.

Newman, Barbara M., and Philip R. Newman, *Infancy & Childhood: Development & Its Contexts.* New York: John Wiley & Sons, 1978.

Oppenheim, Joanne F., *Kids and Play.* New York: Ballantine Books, 1984.

Oppenheim, Joanne, Betty Boegehold and Barbara Brenner, *Raising a Confident Child.* New York: Pantheon Books, 1984.

Osman, Betty B., *Learning Disabilities.* Mount Vernon, N.Y.: Consumers Union, 1979.

Painter, Genevieve, *Teach Your Baby.* New York: Simon & Schuster, 1982.

Payne, Joseph N., ed., *Mathematics Learning in Early Childhood.* Reston, Va.: National Council of Teachers of Mathematics, 1975.

Perino, Sheila C., and Joseph Perino, *Parenting the Gifted.* New York: R. R. Bowker, 1981.

Pulaski, Mary Ann Spencer:
Understanding Piaget. New York: Harper & Row, 1971.
Your Baby's Mind and How It Grows: Piaget's Theory for Parents. New York: Harper & Row, 1981.

Rasmussen, Margaret, ed., *Listen! The Children Speak.* Washington: U.S. National Committee, World Organization for Early Childhood Education, 1979.

Restak, Richard M., M.D., *The Brain.* Toronto: Bantam Books, 1984.

Rose, Steven, *The Conscious Brain.* New York: Alfred A. Knopf, 1973.

Rubin, Richard R., and John J. Fisher III, *Ages Three and Four.* New York: Macmillan, 1982.

Russell, Helen Ross, *A Teacher's Guide: Ten-Minute Field Trips.* Chicago: J. G. Ferguson Publishing Company, 1973.

Scarr, Sandra, Richard A. Weinberg and Ann Levine, *Understanding Development.* San Diego: Harcourt Brace Jovanovich, 1986.

Schickedanz, Judith A., *More Than the ABCs: The Early Stages of Reading and Writing.* Washington: National Association for the Education of Young Children, 1986.

Schneider, Herman, and Nina Schneider:
Science Fun for You in a Minute or Two. New

York: McGraw-Hill, 1975.

Science Fun with a Flashlight. New York: McGraw-Hill, 1975.

Segal, Julius, and Zelda Segal, *Growing Up Smart and Happy.* New York: McGraw-Hill, 1985.

Segal, Marilyn, and Don Adcock, *Just Pretending: Ways to Help Children Grow through Imaginative Play.* Englewood Cliffs, N.J.: Prentice-Hall, 1981.

Sendak, Maurice, *Where the Wild Things Are.* New York: Harper & Row, 1963.

Sharp, Evelyn, *Thinking Is Child's Play.* New York: E. P. Dutton & Co., 1969.

Shilcock, Susan D., and Peter A. Bergson, *Open Connections: The Other Basics.* Bryn Mawr, Pa.: Open Connections, 1980.

Singer, Dorothy G., and Jerome L. Singer, *Make Believe: Games and Activities to Foster Imaginative Play in Young Children.* Glenview, Ill.: Scott, Foresman and Company, 1985.

Singer, Dorothy G., and Tracey A. Revenson, *A Piaget Primer: How a Child Thinks.* New York: Plume, New American Library, 1978.

Singer, Dorothy G., Jerome L. Singer and Diana M. Zuckerman.
Getting the Most Out of TV. Santa Monica, Calif.: Goodyear Publishing Company, 1981.
Teaching Television. New York: Dial Press, 1981.

Sparkman, Brandon, and Ann Carmichael, *Blueprint for a Brighter Child.* New York: McGraw-Hill, 1973.

Sparling, Joseph, and Isabelle Lewis:
Learningames for the First Three Years. New York: Berkley Books, 1979.
Learningames for Threes and Fours. New York: Walker and Company, 1984.

Strang, Ruth, *Helping Your Gifted Child.* New York: E. P. Dutton & Co., 1967.

Sutton-Smith, Brian, ed., *Play and Learning.* New York: Gardner Press, 1979.

Sutton-Smith, Brian, and Shirley Sutton-Smith, *How to Play with Your Children (and When Not to).* New York: Hawthorn/Dutton, 1974.

Vernon, Philip E., *Intelligence: Heredity and Environment.* San Francisco: W. H. Freeman and Company, 1979.

Weininger, Otto, *Play and Education.* Springfield, Ill.: Charles C. Thomas, 1979.

Zaslavsky, Claudia, *Preparing Young Children for Math: A Book of Games.* New York: Schocken Books, 1979.

PERIODICALS

Bell, Trudy E., "Computer Literacy: The Fourth 'R.' " *Personal Computing,* May 1983.

Bowen, Ezra, "Trying to Jump-Start Toddlers." *Time,* April 7, 1986.

Bradley, Robert H., and Bettye M. Caldwell, "The Relation of Infants' Home Environments to Achievement Test Performance in First Grade: A Follow-Up Study." *Child Development,* June 1984.

Bradley, Robert H., Bettye M. Caldwell and Richard Elardo, "Home Environment and Cognitive Development in the First 2 Years." *Developmental Psychology,* Vol. 15, No. 3, 1979.

"Bringing Up Superbaby." *Newsweek,* March 28, 1983.

Copple, Carol, "Shadows and Sand." *Sesame Street Parents' Newsletter,* August 1982.

"The Gifted Child." *Newsweek,* October 23, 1978.

Glazer, Robin Kriegsman, "Let's Pretend." *Working Parents,* June/July 1985.

Naiman, Adeline, "Computers and the Family." *Personal Computing,* September 1985.

Smith, Penny, "Pre-Schoolers Learn at Home." *Creative Computing,* April 1985.

Stechert, Kathryn, "How Much Can a Preschooler Learn from a Computer?" *Better Homes and Gardens,* September 1984.

Watt, Dan, "Software for Preschoolers." *Popular Computing,* March 1985.

OTHER PUBLICATIONS

"Bayley Scales of Infant Development." New York: The Psychological Corporation, 1969.

"HELP Chart," University of Hawaii at Manoa. Palo Alto, Calif.: VORT Corporation, 1979.

Acknowledgments and Picture Credits

The index for this book was prepared by Louise Hedberg. The editors also wish to thank: Robert H. Bradley, University of Arkansas, Little Rock; Roma S. Chandra, M.D., Children's Hospital National Medical Center, Washington, D.C.; Jean Mayo, National Institute of Mental Health, Bethesda, Md.; David P. Weikert, Hyscope Educational Research Foundation, Ypsilanti, Mich.

Credits from left to right are separated by semicolons; from top to bottom by dashes.

Photographs. Cover: Susie Fitzhugh. 7: Joe Rubino. 27: Greg Schaler. 35: Dan Beigel. 46: Beecie Kupersmith. 53-77: Susie Fitzhugh. 79: Dan Beigel. 91: Susie Fitzhugh.

Illustrations. 9: Donald Gates from photo by Jane Jordan. 13: Donald Gates from photo by Vivian Berry. 14-19: Donald Gates from photos by Beecie Kupersmith. 20, 21: Donald Gates from photo by Jane Jordan. 23: Donald Gates from photo by Vivian Berry. 28-33: Robert Hynes from photos by Beecie Kupersmith. 36: Kathe Scherr from photo by Susie Fitzhugh. 41: Larry Paine/Paine, Bluett, Paine, Inc. 42: Kathe Scherr from photo by Beecie Kupersmith, courtesy National Institutes of Health. 47: Kathe Scherr from photo by Jane Jordan. 51: Kathe Scherr from photo by Beecie Kupersmith. 55: Donald Gates from photo by Beecie Kupersmith. 56, 57: Jane Hurd. 62-77: Donald Gates from photos by Susie Fitzhugh. 81, 84, 85: William Hennesy. 92, 93: Marguerite E. Bell from photo by Beecie Kupersmith. 94, 95: Kathe Scherr from photos by Beecie Kupersmith. 96-99: Donald Gates from photos by Beecie Kupersmith. 100, 101: Marguerite E. Bell from photos by Beecie Kupersmith. 102, 103: Donald Gates from photos by Beecie Kupersmith. 104, 105: Marguerite E. Bell from photos by Beecie Kupersmith. 106, 107: Kathe Sherr from photos by Beecie Kupersmith. 108, 109: Marguerite E. Bell from photos by Beecie Kupersmith. 110, 111: Donald Gates from photos by Beecie Kupersmith. 112-117: courtesy Dr. Sylvia Feinburg. 118-121: Kathe Scherr from photos by Beecie Kupersmith. 122-125: Marguerite E. Bell from photos by Beecie Kupersmith. 126: Kathe Scherr from photo by Beecie Kupersmith. 128-132: Marguerite E. Bell from photos by Beecie Kupersmith. 133: Marguerite E. Bell from photos by Jane Jordan. 134-136: Marguerite E. Bell from photos by Beecie Kupersmith. 137: Marguerite E. Bell from photos by Carolyn Rothery.

Index

Symbolic language, 80, 92, 102

T

Talent, 47, 93
Talking, to children, importance of, 12, 100, 101
Taste, activities to develop sense of, 95
Team sports, 130
Telephone, made from cans, 125
Television:
  commercials, 25
  confusing for young children, 23-24
  guidelines for watching, 25, 26
  Parent to Parent on, 27
  violence in, 24-25
Testing and evaluation of children, 40-45
  at early age, 48
  for giftedness, 48
  hearing and language, 86-87
  of learning-disabled children, 82, 84
  for retardation, 89
  of vision, 87
  See also IQ tests
Tests:
  achievement, 11
  of creativity, 44
  dynamic assessment, 44
  IQ, 40-45, 54
Thought process, of preschoolers, *28-33*
  See also Cognitive development; Cognitive skills;
    Memory; Mental abilities; Reasoning

Throwing and catching a ball, *129,* 133
Thyroid gland, malfunction of, 88
Time, child's sense of, 33, 58, 59, 70, 72
Toddlers:
  reading to, 102
  toys for, 93
Toys:
  discovering new uses for, 96-97
  for infants and toddlers, 93
  providing, 90, 93
  selecting appropriate, 64, 68, 70, 72, 74, 76
  storing, 18, 93
Tracing:
  bodies, *111*
  pictures and words, *105*
  shadows, *123*
Train ride, *109*
Treasure-hunt games, *66, 68*
Trial and error, as part of learning process, 13, 59,
    60, 70, *71,* 72, 76
Tumbling, 133
Tunnels, 133
Tunnel vision, 88
Twenty questions, 99
Twins, test scores of fraternal and identical, 34, 38-
    39
Typewriter, and letter recognition, 103

V

Verbal skills:

enhancing, 101
and reading readiness, 102
Videocassettes, selecting for children, 23, 25
Violence, on television, 24-25
Vision:
  development of, 64, 66
  impairment of, 87-88
Visual arts, activities that foster, *110-111*
Vocabulary, growth and development, 100, 102,
    103
  See also Language skills
Vocalizing, activities, 100

W

Walking, 70
Water, learning about, 124
Water play, 134
Weather games, 108
Weight, learning about, 119
What if? game, 97
What's different? game, 99
What's in the picture? game, *101*
What's next? activity, 98
Where the Wild Things Are, 29
Windup toys, *128-129*
Writing skills, activities that develop, *104-105,* 126-
    127

Z

Zero, learning about concept of, 120-121